1990 - 2000
A Decade of
BROADWAY & CABARET SONGS

Project Manager: Sy Feldman
Art Design: Carmen Fortunato
Cast Photos: Photofest (unless otherwise indicated)

© 2000 WARNER BROS. PUBLICATIONS
All Rights Reserved

Any duplication, adaptation or arrangement of the compositions
contained in this collection requires the written consent of the Publisher.
No part of this book may be photocopied or reproduced in any way without permission.
Unauthorized uses are an infringement of the U.S. Copyright Act and are punishable by law.

SHOW HIGHLIGHTS & HISTORY

CLOSER THAN EVER
Opened: 11/06/1989
Cherry Lane Theatre
Off-Broadway: 288 Performances

Music: David Shire
Lyrics: Richard Maltby, Jr.
Producer: Janet Brenner; Michael Gill; Daryl Roth
Director: Richard Maltby, Jr.; Steven Scott Smith
Choreographer: Marcia Milgrom Dodge

Cast: Brent Barrett, Patrick Scott Brady, Sally Mayes, Richard Muenz, Lynn Wintersteller

James Naughton

CITY OF ANGELS
Opened: 12/11/1989
Virginia Theatre
Broadway: 878 Performances

Music: Cy Coleman
Lyrics: David Zippel
Book: Larry Gelbart
Producer: Roger Berlin; Jujamcyn Theaters; The Shubert Organization; Suntory International Corp; Nick Vanoff
Director: Michael Blakemore
Choreographer: Walter Painter

Cast: Rene Auberjonois, Gregg Edelman, Randy Graff, Dee Hoty, Kay McClelland, James Naughton, Scott Waara, Rachel York

LATE NITE COMIC
Opened: 10/15/87
Ritz Theatre
Broadway: 4 Performances

Music & Lyrics: Brian Gari
Book: Allan Knee
Producer: Rory Rosegarten
Musical Director: Gregory J. Dlugos
Choreographer: Dennis Dennehy

Cast: Robert LuPone, Teresa Tracy

ASSASSINS
Opened: 01/27/1991
Playwrights Horizons Theatre
Off-Broadway: 25 Performances

Music & Lyrics: Stephen Sondheim
Book: John Weidman
Producer: Playwrights Horizons
Director: Jerry Zaks
Choreographer: D.J. Giagni

Cast: Jace Alexander, Patrick Cassidy, Joy Franz, Victor Garber, Greg Germann, Annie Golden, Lyn Greene, Jonathan Hadary, John Jellison, Eddie Korbich, Terrence Mann, Debra Monk, Marcus Olson, William Parry, Michael Shulman, Lee Wilkof

Mandy Patinkin and Daisy Eagan

THE SECRET GARDEN
Opened: 04/25/1991
St. James Theatre
Broadway: 706 Performances

Music: Lucy Simon
Lyrics: Marsha Norman
Book: Marsha Norman
Producer: Dodger Productions; Jujamcyn Theaters; Heidi Landesman; Frederic H. Mayerson; Rick Steiner, TV ASAHI; Elizabeth Williams
Director: Susan H. Schulman

Cast: Daisy Eagan, Alison Fraser, Rebecca Judd, Rebecca Luker, John Cameron Mitchell, Mandy Patinkin, Tom Toner, Robert Westenberg

CHILDREN OF EDEN
Opened: 01/08/1991
Prince Edward Theatre
London: 103 Performances

Music & Lyrics: Stephen Schwartz
Book: John Caird
Producer: Atlantic Overtures; Children of Eden, Ltd.
Director: John Caird
Choreographer: Matthew Bourne

Cast: Shion Abdillah, Adrian Beaumont, Earlene Bentley, Kevin Colson, Ramilles Corbin, Richard Lloyd-King, Ken Page, Shezwae Powell, Frances Ruffelle, Ray Shell, Martin Smith, Ashley Walters

Keith Carradine and Dee Hoty

THE WILL ROGERS FOLLIES

Opened: 05/01/1991
Palace Theatre
Broadway: 963 Performances

Music: Cy Coleman
Lyrics: Betty Comden; Adolph Green
Book: Peter Stone
Producer: Pierre Cosette; Sam Crothers; Stewart F. Lane; James M. Nederlander; Martin Richards; Max Weitzenhoffer
Director: Tommy Tune
Choreographer: Tommy Tune

Cast: Bonnie Brackney, Tom Brackney, Vince Bruce, Keith Carradine, Dee Hoty, Cady Huffman, Dick Latessa, Gregory Peck*, Paul Ukena, Jr.

*Voice on tape only

NICK & NORA

Opened: 12/08/1991
Marquis Theatre
Broadway: 9 Performances

Music: Charles Strouse
Lyrics: Richard Maltby, Jr.
Book: Arthur Laurents
Producer: Terry Allen Kramer; Elizabeth Ireland McCann; Charlene Nederlander; James M. Nederlander; Daryl Roth
Director: Arthur Laurents
Choreographer: Tina Paul

Cast: Christine Baranski, Barry Bostwick, Jeff Brooks, Joanna Gleason, Michael Lombard, Debra Monk, Kathy Morath, Kip Niven, Faith Prince, Remak Ramsay, Riley, Chris Sarandon, Thom Sesma

BALANCING ACT

Opened: 06/15/1992
Westside Theatre
Off-Broadway: 56 Performances

Music & Lyrics: Dan Goggin
Book: Dan Goggin
Producer: N.N.N. Company
Director: Dan Goggin; Tony Parise
Choreographer: Dan Goggin; Tony Parise

Cast: J.B. Adams, Diane Fratantoni, Suzanne Hevner, Christine Toy, Craig Wells

PASSION

Opened: 05/09/1994
Plymouth Theatre
Broadway: 280 Performances

Music & Lyrics: Stephen Sondheim
Book: James Lapine
Producer: Roger Berlind; Capital Cities/ABC; Scott Rudin; The Shubert Organization
Director: James Lapine

Cast: Tom Aldredge, Gibby Brand, George Dvorsky, Gregg Edelman, Colleen Fitzpatrick, Cris Groenendaal, Juliet Lambert, Frank Lombardi, Marin Mazzie, Donna Murphy, Marcus Olson, William Parry, Matthew Poretta, Francis Ruivivar, Jere Shea, John Leslie Wolfe

Kevin Ramsey and Pamela Isaacs

THE LIFE

Opened: 04/26/1997
Ethel Barrymore Theatre
Broadway: 465 Performances

Music: Cy Coleman
Lyrics: Ira Gasman
Book: David Newman; Ira Gasman; Cy Coleman
Producer: Roger Berlind; Martin Richards; Cy Coleman; Sam Crothers
Director: Michael Blakemore
Choreographer: Joey McKneely

Cast: Pamela Isaacs, Kevin Ramsey, Lillias White, Chuck Cooper, Bellamy Young, Vernel Bagneris, Rich Hebert, Gordon Joseph Weiss, Sam Harris

DIVAS OF CABARET

Terrence Mann and Christine Andreas

THE SCARLET PIMPERNEL

Opened: 11/09/1997
The Minskoff Theatre
Broadway: 843 Performances

Music:	Frank Wildhorn
Lyrics:	Nan Knighton
Book:	Nan Knighton
Director:	Peter Hunt (Revised production: Robert Longbottom)
Producer:	Pierre Cossette; Bill Haber; Hallmark Entertainment; Ted Forstmann; Kathleen Raitt
Choreographer:	Adam Pelty (Revised production: Robert Longbottom)

Cast: Christine Andreas, Pamela Barrell, Ed Dixon, Philip Hoffman, Terrence Mann, Gilles Schiasson, Douglas Sills

RAGTIME

Opened: 01/18/1998
Ford Center for the Performing Arts
Broadway: 834 Performances

Music:	Stephen Flaherty
Lyrics:	Lynn Ahrens
Book:	Terrence McNally
Producer:	Livent, Inc.
Director:	Frank Galati
Choreographer:	Graciela Daniele

Cast: Jim Corti, Peter Friedman, Tommy Hollis, Mark Jacoby, Judy Kaye, Marin Mazzie, Audra McDonald, Brian Stokes Mitchell, Lynette Perry, Steven Sutcliffe

Audra McDonald and Anthony Crivello

MARIE CHRISTINE

Opened: 12/02/1999
Center Theater at the Vivian Beaumont
Broadway: 46 Performances

Music & Lyrics:	Michael John LaChiusa
Producer:	André Bishop; Bernard Gersten
Director & Choreographer:	Graciela Daniele

Cast: Sherry Boone, Anthony Crivello, Shawn Elliott, Kim Huber, Mark Lotito, Michael McCormick, Audra McDonald, Janet Metz, Vivian Reed, Mary Testa

MARGARET WHITING

Margaret Whiting provides great rewards to all of us through her singing. She was "born to make music," and few careers in American popular music equal hers; fewer still surpass it. She has recorded more than five hundred songs and has earned twelve Gold Records, meaning sales of 500,000 copies each. She is a singer who has introduced some of the greatest pop standards of all time: "That Old Black Magic," "Come Rain or Come Shine," "Far Away Places," "It Might as Well Be Spring," "A Tree in the Meadow," among many others, and of course a song that will forever be associated with her, "Moonlight in Vermont."

Margaret Whiting came to her love of and life in music quite honestly. Her father, Richard Whiting, was a legendary composer of such major works as "Beyond the Blue Horizon," "'Til We Meet Again," "Too Marvelous for Words," and "Hooray for Hollywood."

Coached by famed lyricist Johnny Mercer, she recorded for Mercer's company, Capitol Records. As a cabaret performer, she headlined at Rainbow & Stars, the Algonquin, the Russian Tea Room, and Tavern on the Green, as well as the Hollywood Roosevelt Cine Grill and Pizza in the Park in London. She has also appeared throughout the country in major musical comedies and plays, starring in productions of *Gypsy, Pal Joey,* and *Call Me Madam.*

PORTIA NELSON

Legendary cabaret singer, Portia Nelson, has five Columbia albums and four solo albums and is included in the Smithsonian recordings of great popular singers, Cole Porter, and Kurt Weill. Her recent CDs include *Sunday in New York, Let Me Love You* (Bart Howard Songs), and *This Life . . . Her Songs and Her Friends.*

Also a composer-lyricist, Nelson received her most recent honor when Marilyn Horne sang her song, "Make a Rainbow," at President Clinton's inauguration.

Her book, *There's a Hole in My Sidewalk,* is in its third edition and is a staple in self-recovery groups around the world. Her poem, "Autobiography in Five Short Chapters," is now in poster form and used by therapists and self-help centers worldwide.

As an actress, Nelson is most remembered as Sister Berthe in the film *The Sound of Music* and as Mrs. Gurney for eight years on "All My Children."

She has been honored by Women in Film (of which she is a founder), ASCAP, the Mabel Mercer Foundation, the Utah Centennial Celebration '96 (where Lady Margaret Thatcher presented medals), and Weber College as a Distinguished Alumnae. Backstage News honored her with their Lifetime Achievement Award in March 1996.

CONTENTS

Title	Show or Performer	Page
AS I REMEMBER HIM	*NANCY LAMOTT*	82
CAN'T TEACH MY OLD HEART NEW TRICKS	*MARGARET WHITING*	78
CLOSER THAN EVER	*CLOSER THAN EVER*	6
THE COFFEE SHOPPE	*MARGARET WHITING*	73
CONFESSION OF A NEW YORKER	*PORTIA NELSON*	64
EVERYBODY'S GIRL	*STEEL PIER*	55
GOODBYE, MY LOVE	*RAGTIME*	48
HAPPINESS	*PASSION*	37
A HARD TIME TO BE SINGLE	*A HARD TIME TO BE SINGLE*	10
THE HUMAN HEART	*ONCE ON THIS ISLAND*	14
I NEVER WANTED TO LOVE YOU	*FALSETTOS*	154
I'D RATHER BE SAILING	*A NEW BRAIN*	132
LATE NITE COMIC	*LATE NITE COMIC*	128
LIFE IS A BALANCING ACT	*BALANCING ACT*	162
LILY'S EYES	*THE SECRET GARDEN*	21
MAKE A RAINBOW	*PORTIA NELSON/MARILYN HORNE*	28
MARRIED LIFE	*NICK & NORA*	139
MY FRIEND	*THE LIFE*	32
NEVER MET A MAN I DIDN'T LIKE	*THE WILL ROGERS FOLLIES*	142
THE OLDEST PROFESSION	*THE LIFE*	120
STOP, TIME	*BIG*	85
UNWORTHY OF YOUR LOVE	*ASSASSINS*	88
WAY BACK TO PARADISE	*MARIE CHRISTINE*	176
WHAT MORE CAN I SAY?	*FALSETTOS*	96
WHEELS OF A DREAM	*RAGTIME*	166
WHEN I LOOK AT YOU	*THE SCARLET PIMPERNEL*	101
A WORLD WITHOUT YOU	*CHILDREN OF EDEN*	114
YOU ARE MY HOME	*THE SCARLET PIMPERNEL*	150
YOU'RE NOTHING WITHOUT ME	*CITY OF ANGELS*	106

CLOSER THAN EVER

Lyrics by
RICHARD MALTBY, JR.

Music by
DAVID SHIRE

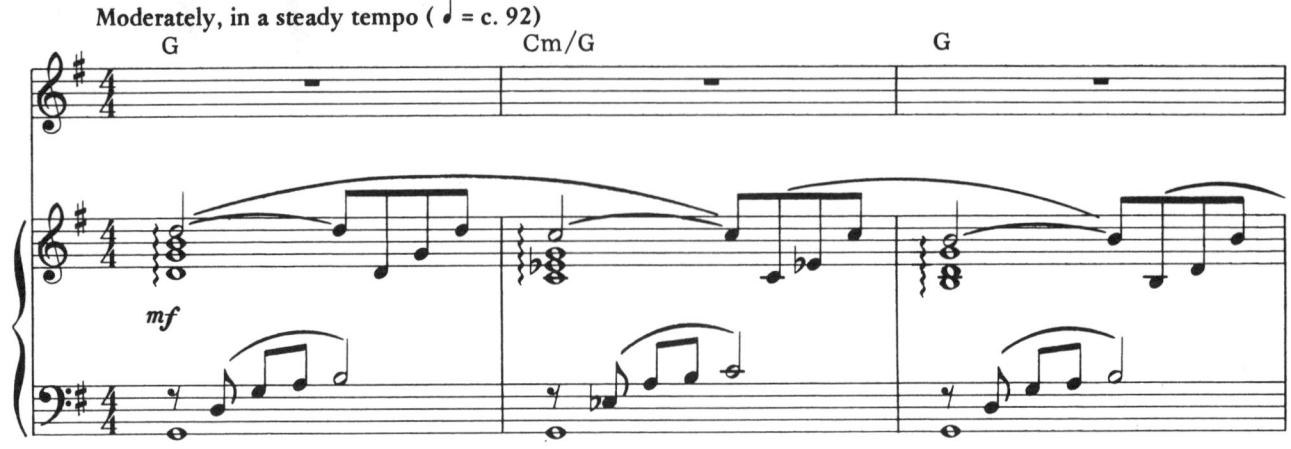

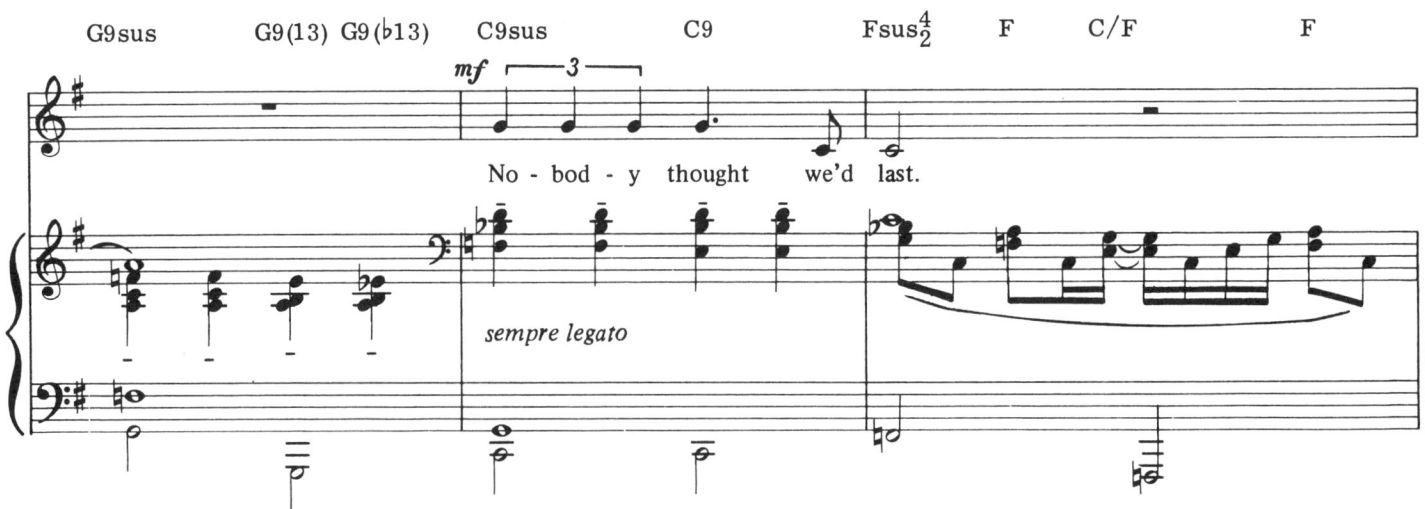

No-bod-y thought we'd last.

Good thing we nev-er knew it. It's fun-ny how af-ter all these years We're

© 1989 PROGENY MUSIC, WARNER-TAMERLANE PUBLISHING CORP.
LONG POND MUSIC and WB MUSIC CORP.
All Rights Administered by WARNER-TAMERLANE PUBLISHING CORP. and WB MUSIC CORP.
All Rights Reserved

Closer Than Ever - 4 - 4

A HARD TIME TO BE SINGLE

Words and Music by
BRIAN GARI

1. Walked home from a par-ty where most girls were at-tached, and just like Lau-rel and Har-dy, they real-ly seemed mis-matched. It's
2. And ev-'ry-one's in-volved now ex-cept a pre-cious few, 'cause no one's tak-ing chanc-es there's dan-ger if you do. And
3. And may-be he'll dis-cov-er that is, if he is bright, that if you have a lov-er, hold on ex-tra tight. 'Cause

A Hard Time to Be Single - 4 - 1

© 1991 TENACITY MUSIC (ASCAP) and FOXBOROUGH JR. MUSIC (ASCAP)
All Rights Reserved

THE HUMAN HEART

Words by
LYNN AHRENS

MUSIC BY
STEPHEN FLAHERTY

The Human Heart - 7 - 1

© 1990 WB MUSIC CORP., WARNER-TAMERLANE PUBLISHING CORP., HILLSDALE MUSIC, INC. and DORMONT MUSIC
All Rights on behalf of HILLSDALE MUSIC, INC. Administered by WB MUSIC CORP.
All Rights on behalf of DORMONT MUSIC Administered by WARNER-TAMERLANE PUBLISHING CORP.
All Rights Reserved

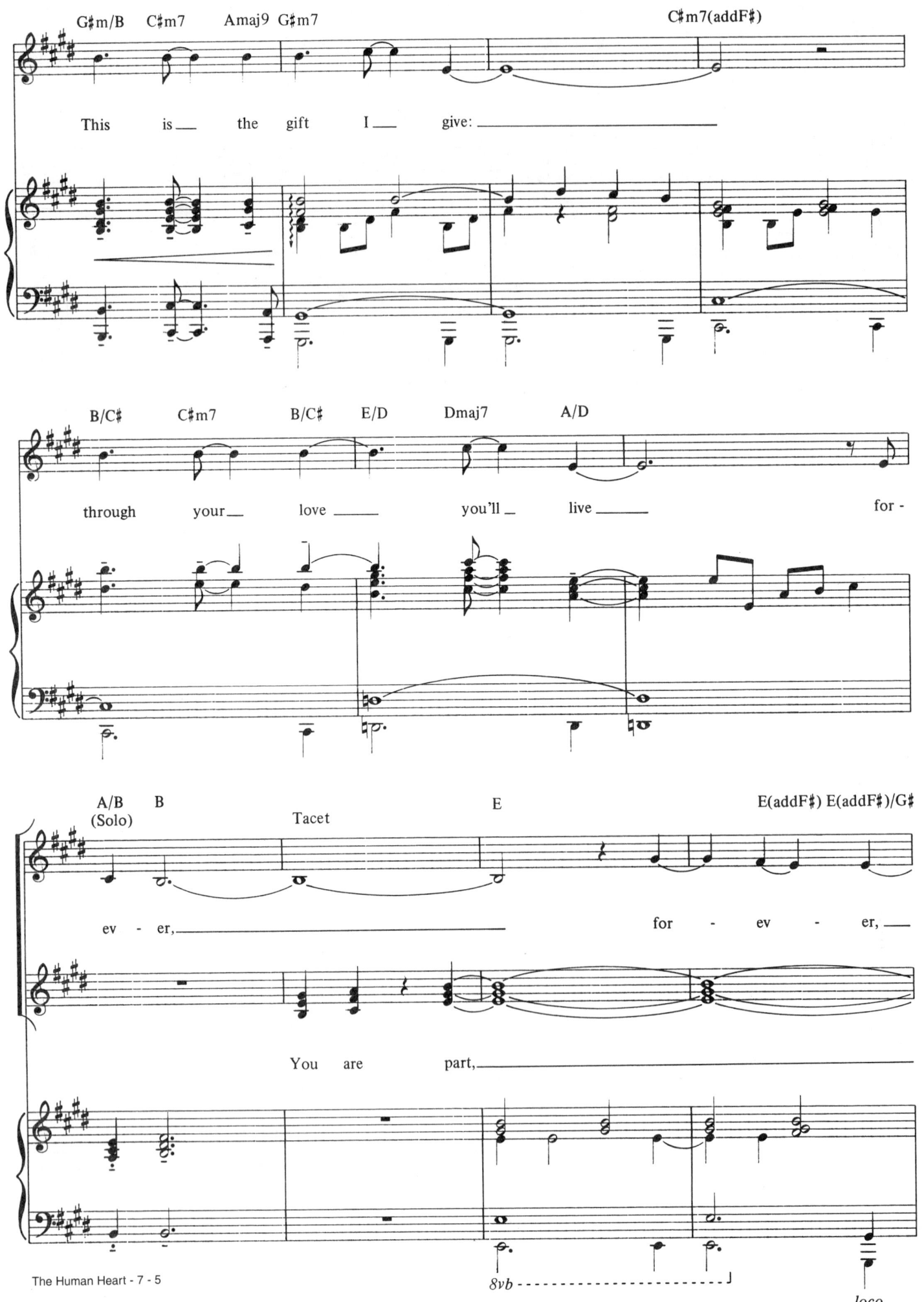

LILY'S EYES

Lyrics by
MARSHA NORMAN

Music by
LUCY SIMON

Calmly
DR. CRAVEN: Strange-ly qui-et, but now the storm sim-ply rests to strike a-gain.

p molto legato
with pedal

C: Stand-ing, wait-ing, I think of her; I think of

C: her.

ARCHIE: Strange this Mar-y, she leaves the room, yet re-mains; she lin-gers on.

Lily's Eyes - 7 - 1

Piano arrangement by Michael Kosarin

© 1991, 1992 ABCDE PUBLISHING LTD. and CALOUGIE MUSIC
All rights administered by WB MUSIC CORP.
All Rights Reserved

MAKE A RAINBOW

Music and Lyrics by
PORTIA NELSON

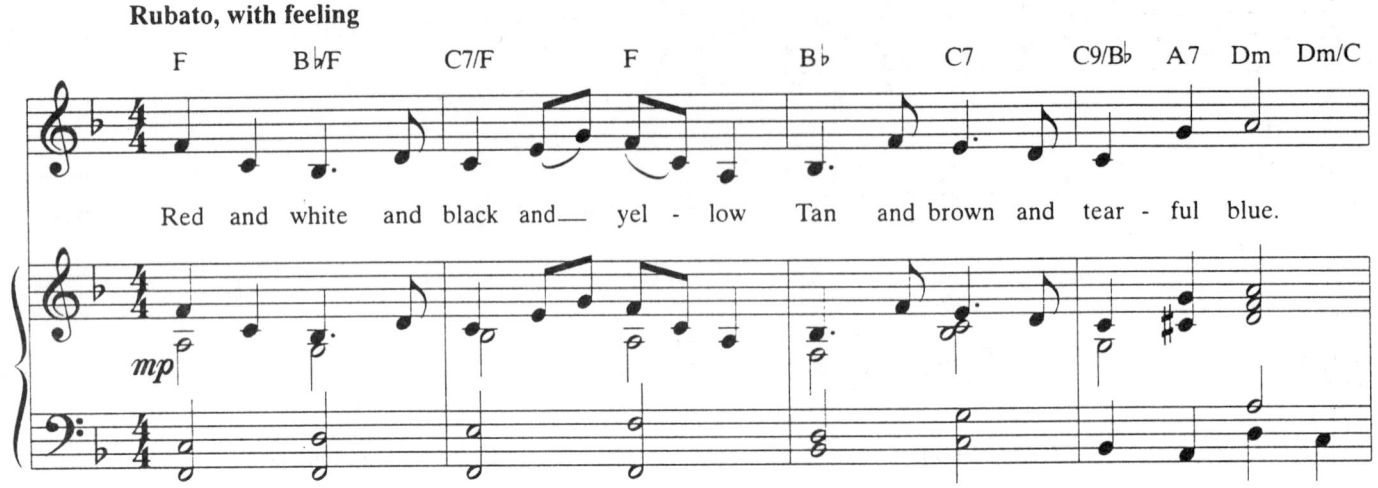

Red and white and black and yellow Tan and brown and tearful blue.

These are the colors of children ev-'ry-where Just like me and you.

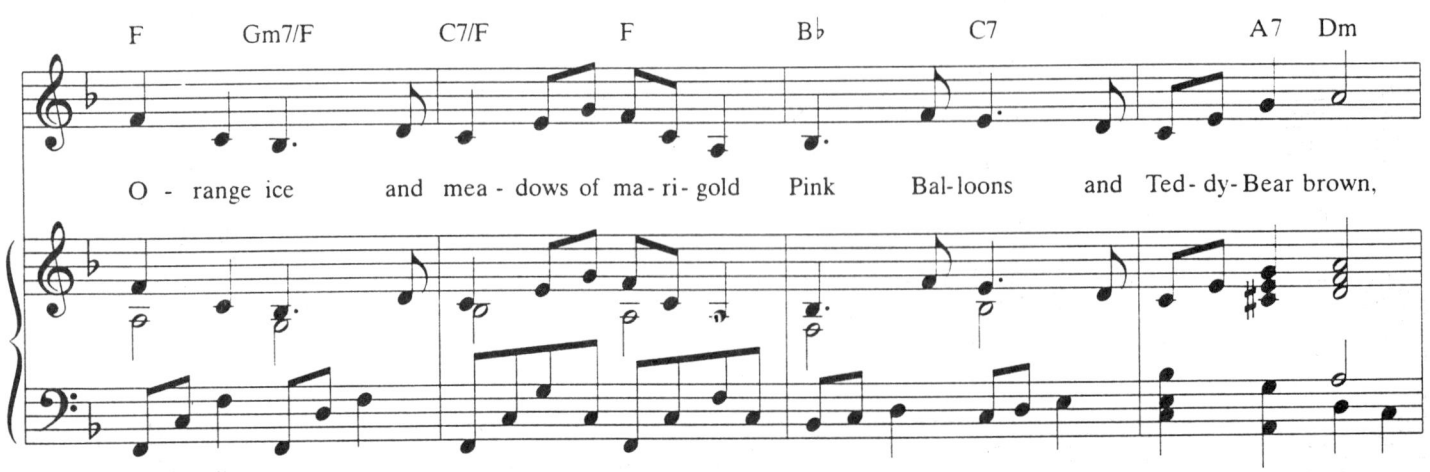

Orange ice and meadows of marigold Pink Balloons and Teddy-Bear brown,

© 1969, 1993 WB MUSIC CORP. and DANNEL MUSIC PUBLISHING
All rights administered by WB MUSIC CORP.
All Rights Reserved

Make a Rainbow - 4 - 2

MY FRIEND

Music by
CY COLEMAN

Lyrics by
IRA GASMAN

© 1996 NOTABLE MUSIC CO., INC. (ASCAP)
This Arrangement © 1997 NOTABLE MUSIC CO., INC.
All Rights Administered by WB MUSIC CORP. (ASCAP)
All Rights Reserved

HAPPINESS

Music and Lyrics by
STEPHEN SONDHEIM

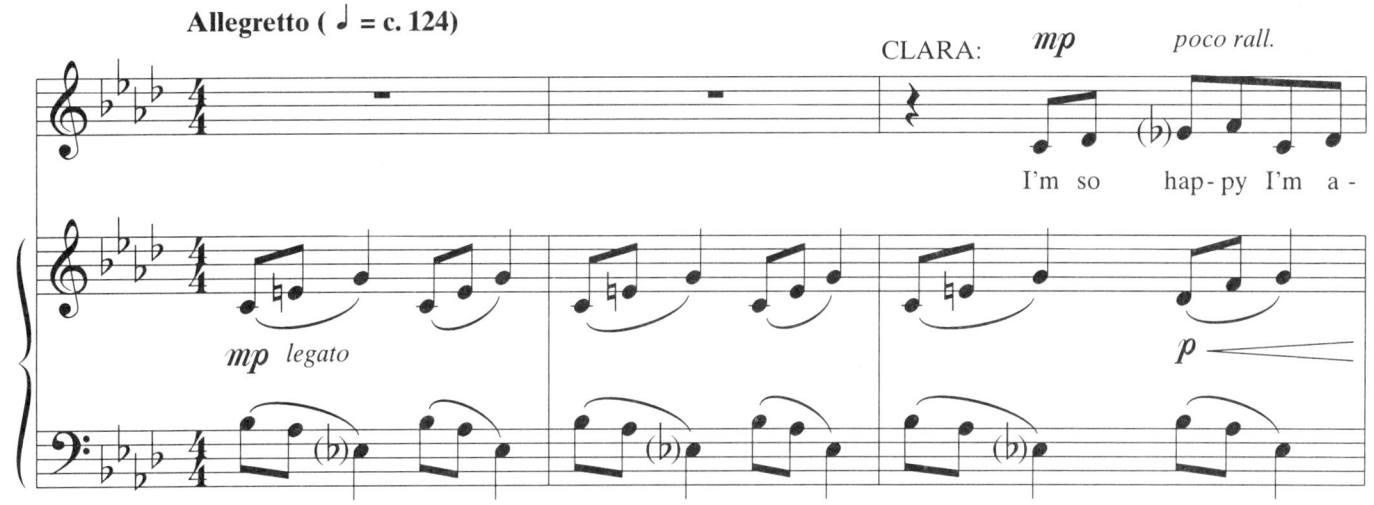

I'm so hap-py I'm a-

fraid I'll die Here in your arms. What would you do if I

died-- Like this-- Right now, Here in your arms?

© 1994 RILTING MUSIC, INC.
All Rights Administered by WB MUSIC CORP.
All Rights Reserved

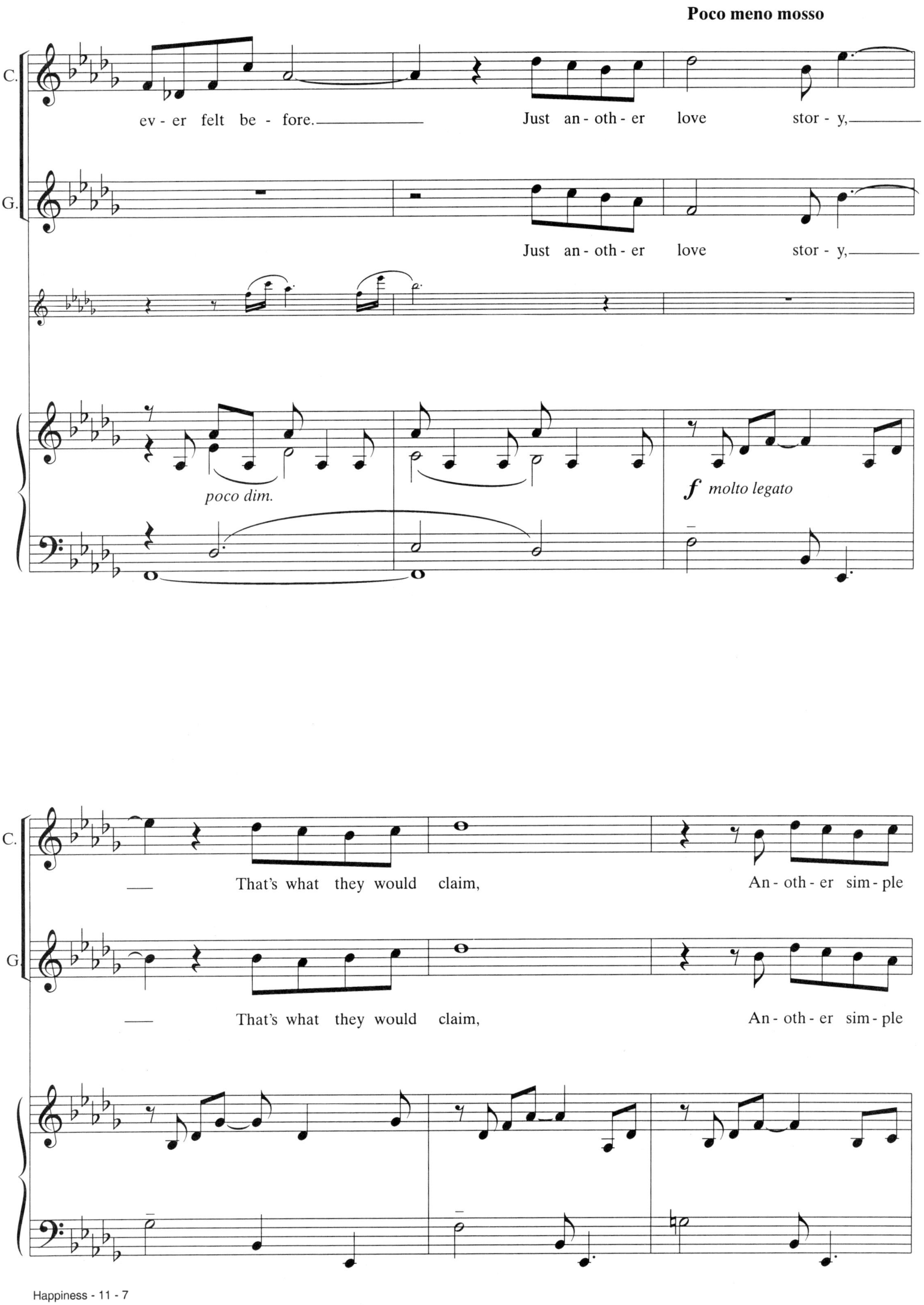
Poco meno mosso
C.
G.
ev - er felt be - fore.
Just an - oth - er love stor - y,
Just an - oth - er love stor - y,
poco dim.
f molto legato
That's what they would claim,
An - oth - er sim - ple
That's what they would claim,
An - oth - er sim - ple

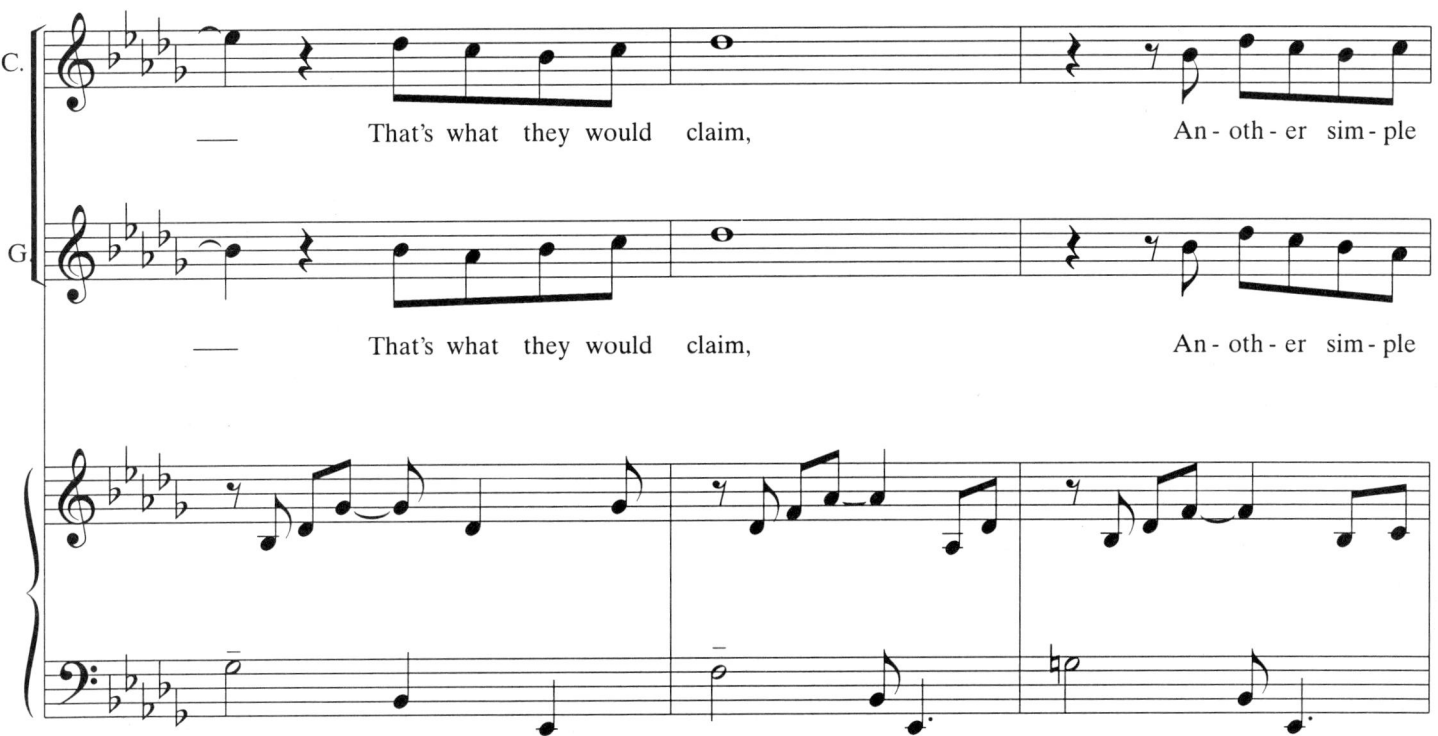

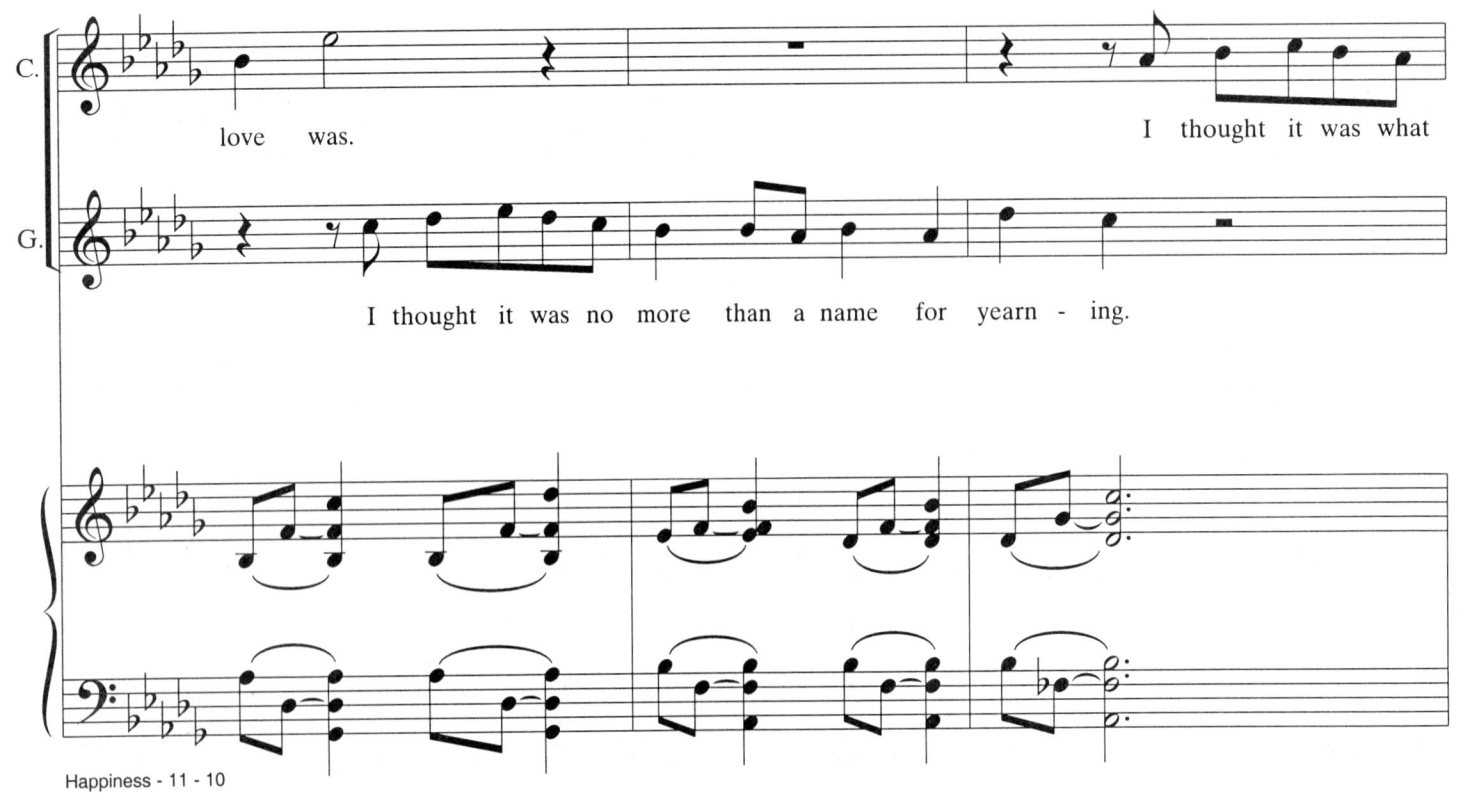

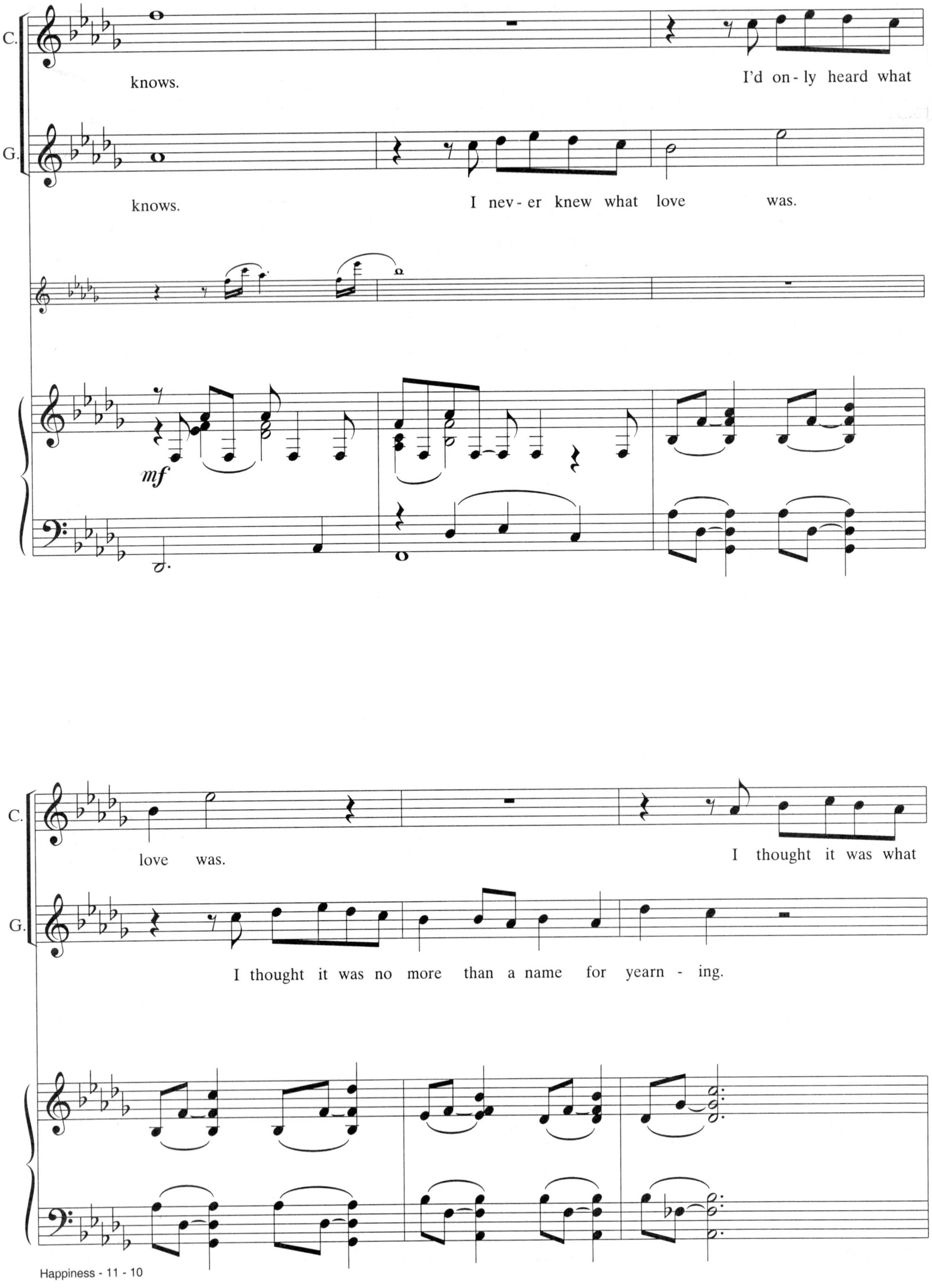
C.
knows.
I'd on - ly heard what
G.
knows.
I nev - er knew what love was.
mf
C.
love was.
I thought it was what
G.
I thought it was no more than a name for yearn - ing.

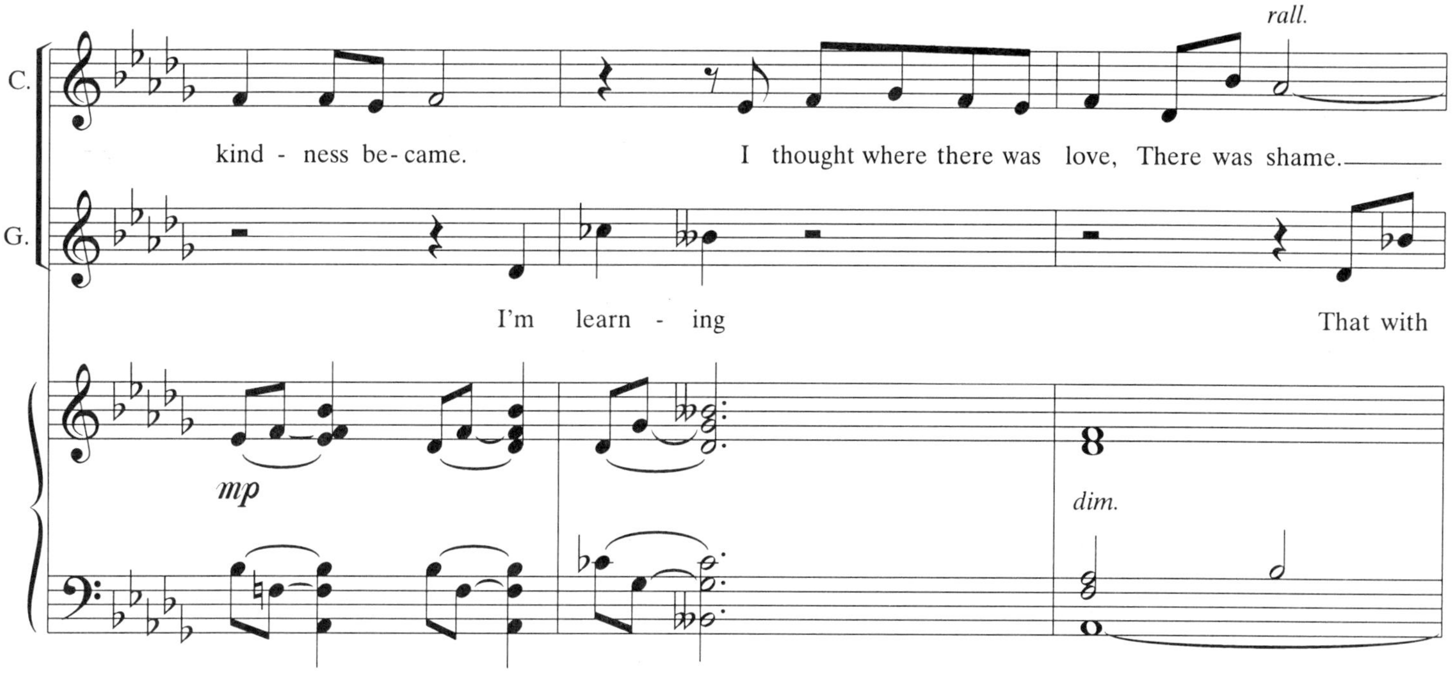
rall.
C.
kind - ness be- came. I thought where there was love, There was shame.
G.
I'm learn - ing That with
mp
dim.

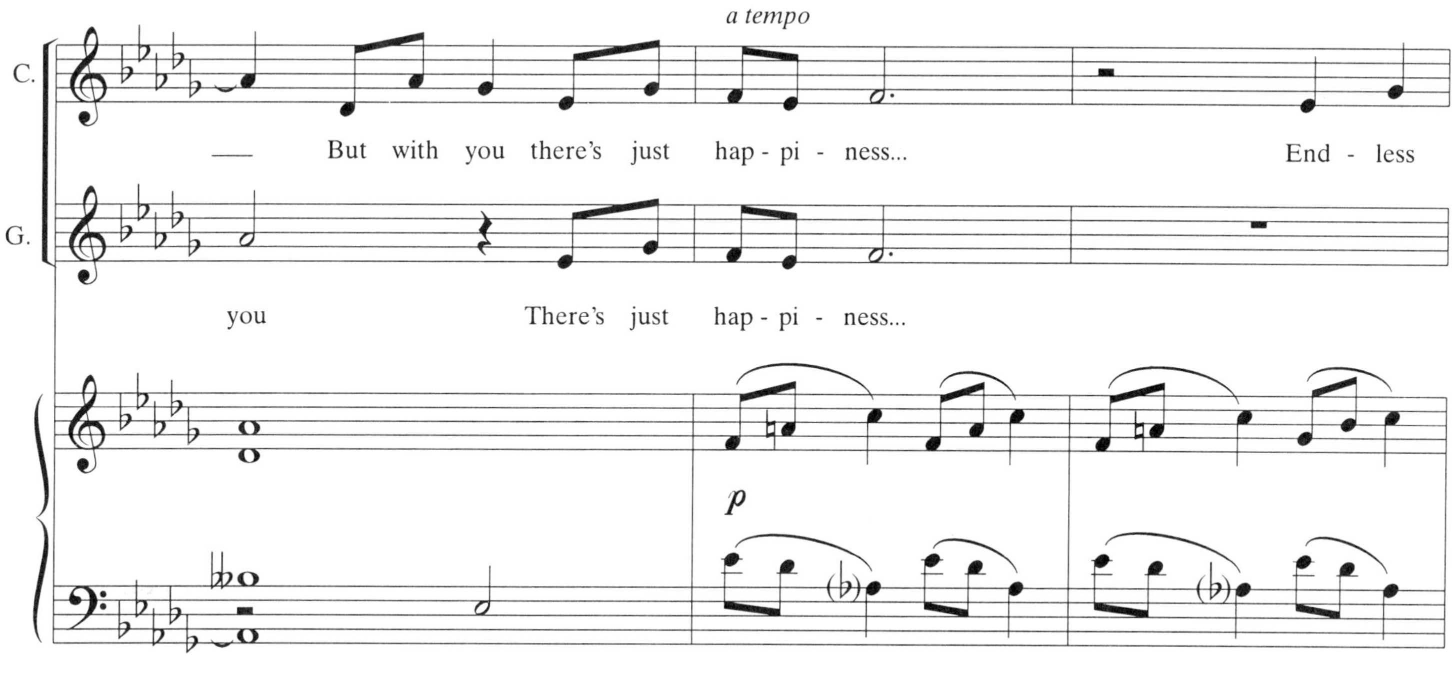
a tempo
C.
But with you there's just hap - pi - ness... End - less
G.
you There's just hap - pi - ness...
p

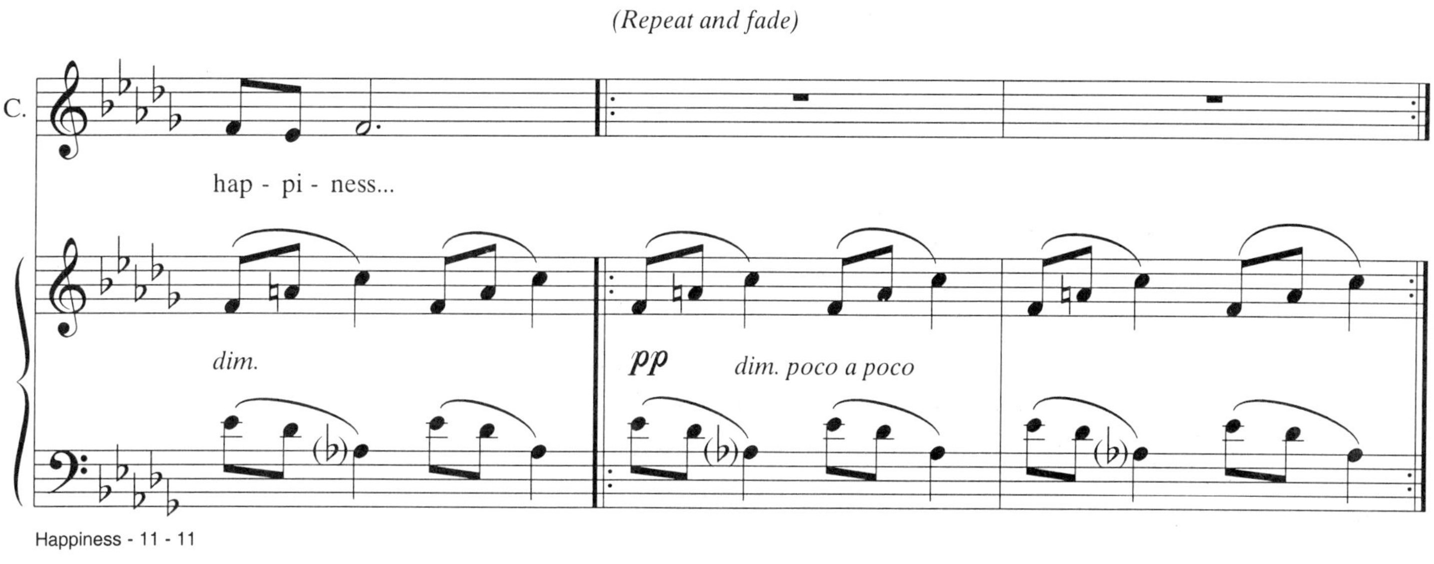
(Repeat and fade)
C.
hap - pi - ness...
dim.
pp
dim. poco a poco

GOODBYE, MY LOVE

Lyrics by
LYNN AHRENS

Music by
STEPHEN FLAHERTY

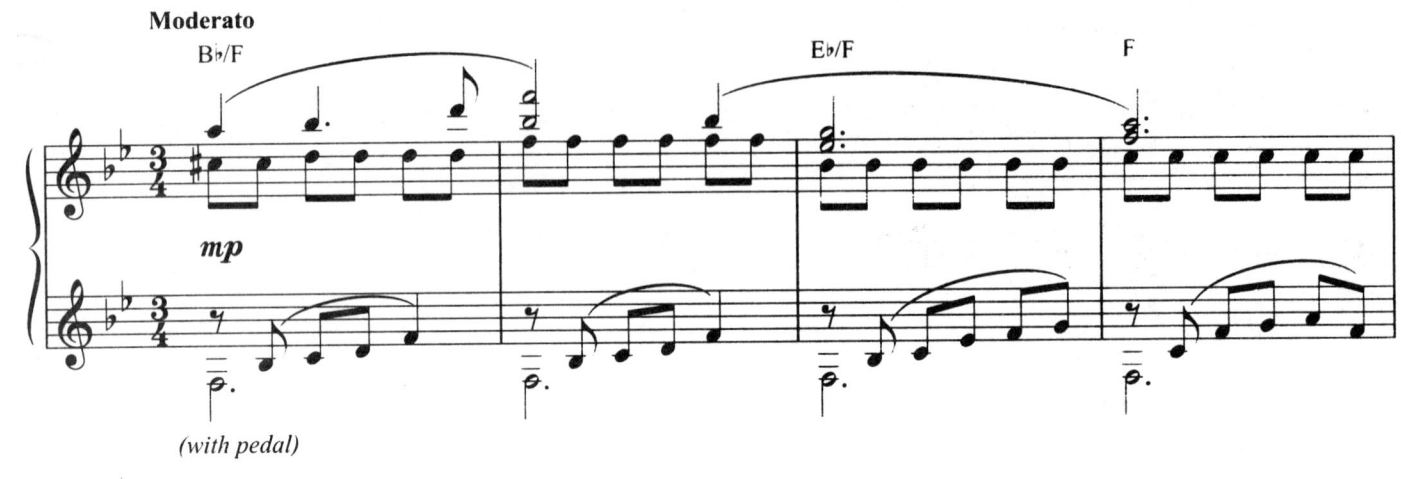
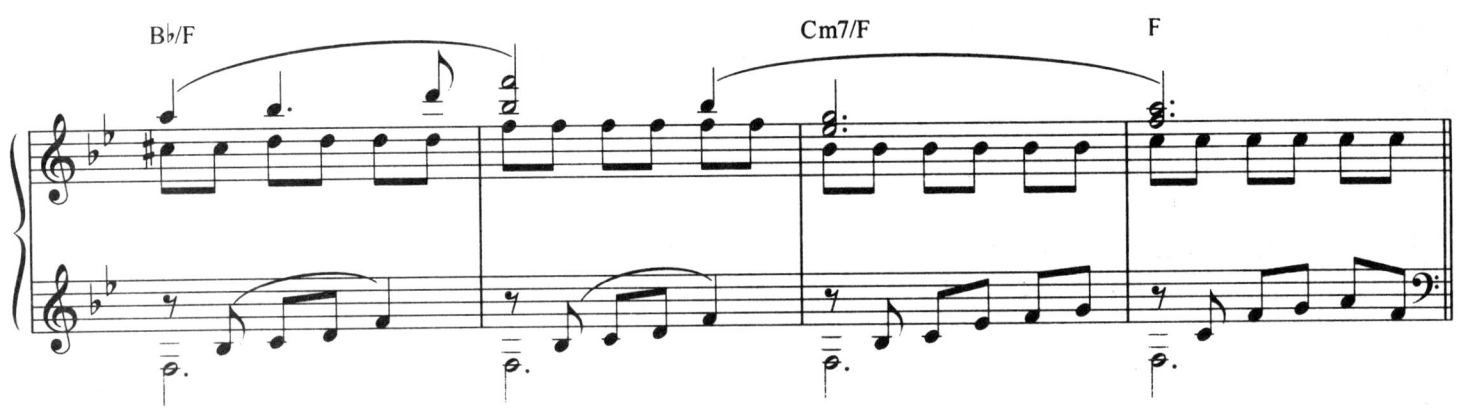

Goodbye, my love. God bless you.

© 1996, 1997 WB MUSIC CORP., PEN AND PERSEVERANCE and HILLSDALE MUSIC, INC.
All Rights Administered by WB MUSIC CORP.
All Rights Reserved including Public Performance for Profit

EVERYBODY'S GIRL

Lyrics by
FRED EBB

Music by
JOHN KANDER

Everybody's Girl - 9 - 1

© 1997 KANDER & EBB, INC. (BMI)
All Rights Administered by WARNER-TAMERLANE PUBLISHING CORP.
All Rights Reserved

CONFESSION OF A NEW YORKER
(Hate—Love New York)

Music and Lyrics by
PORTIA NELSON

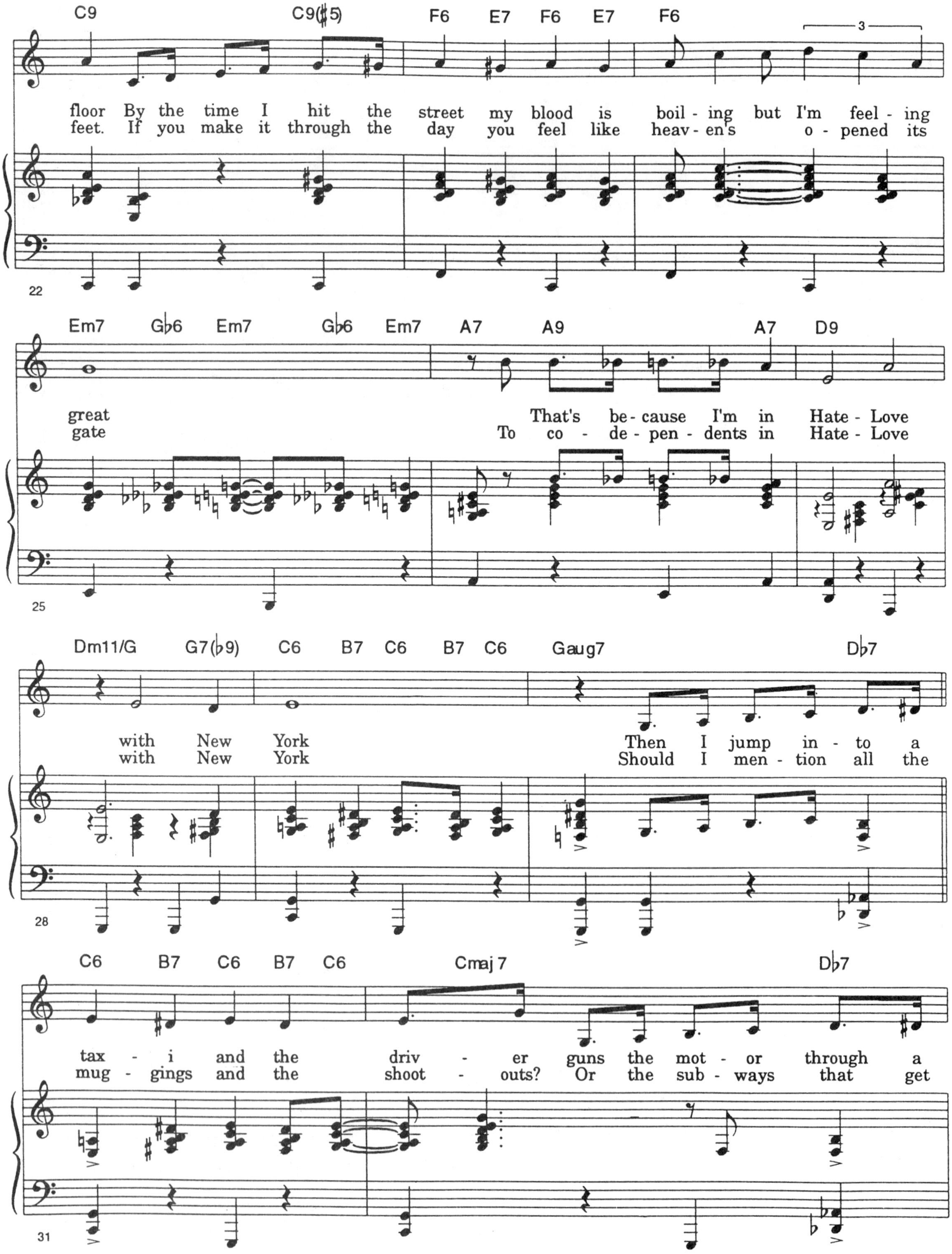
C9 C9(♯5) F6 E7 F6 E7 F6
floor By the time I hit the street my blood is boil - ing but I'm feel - ing
feet. If you make it through the day you feel like heav - en's o - pened its
22
Em7 G♭6 Em7 G♭6 Em7 A7 A9 A7 D9
great That's be - cause I'm in Hate - Love
gate To co - de - pen - dents in Hate - Love
25
Dm11/G G7(♭9) C6 B7 C6 B7 C6 Gaug7 D♭7
with New York Then I jump in - to a
with New York Should I men - tion all the
28
C6 B7 C6 B7 C6 Cmaj7 D♭7
tax - i and the driv - er guns the mot - or through a
mug - gings and the shoot - outs? Or the sub - ways that get
31

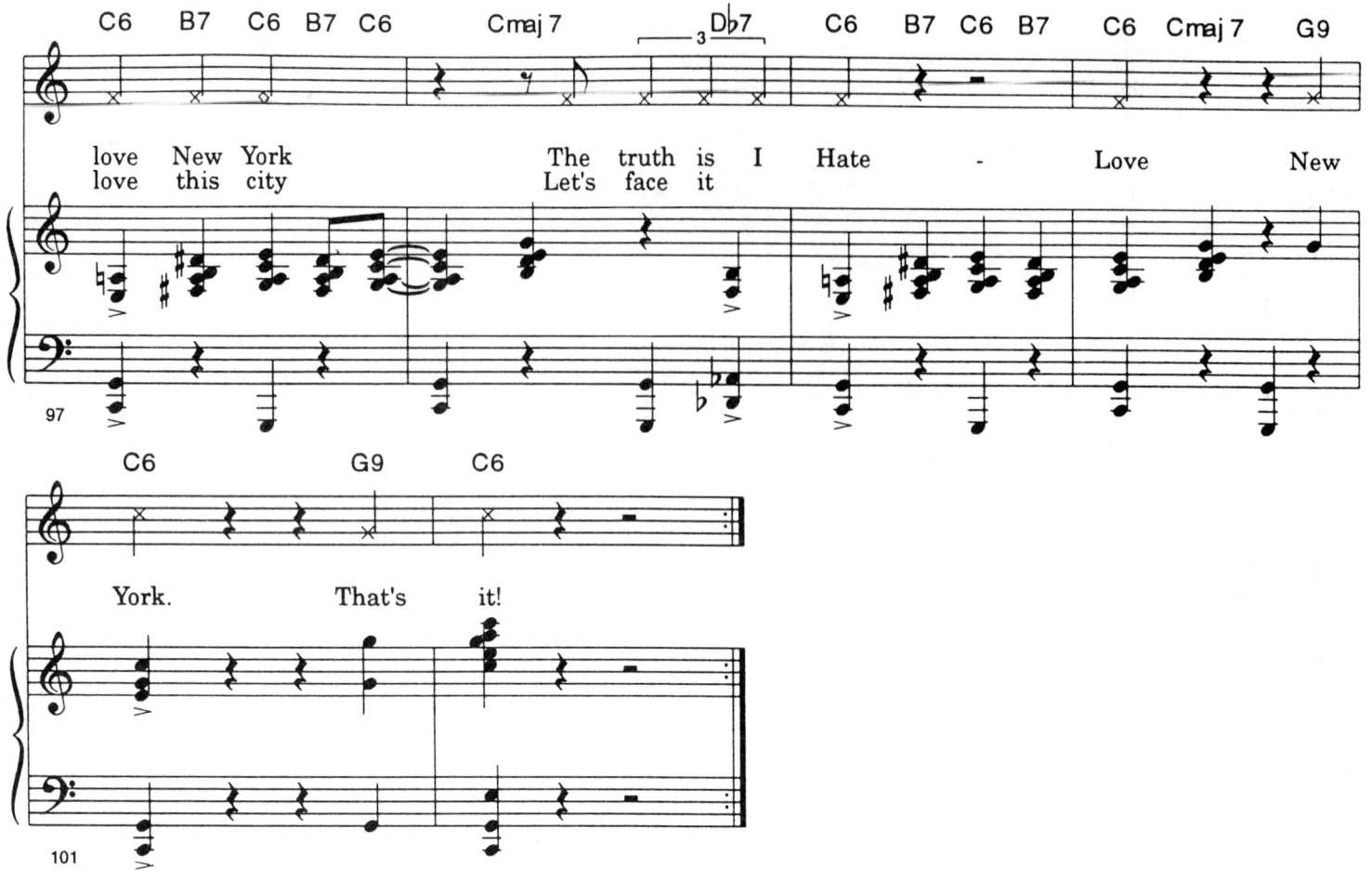

THE COFFEE SHOPPE

Words and Music by
BRIAN GARI

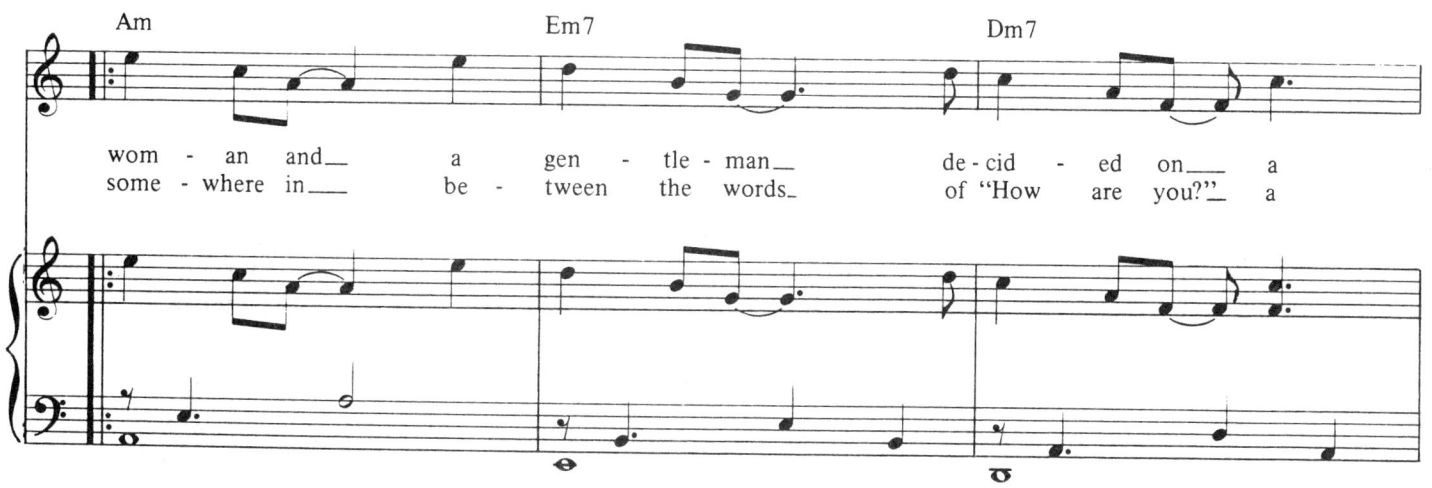

The Coffee Shoppe - 5 - 1

© 1991 Tenacity Music (ASCAP) and FOXBOROUGH JR. MUSIC (ASCAP)
All Rights Reserved

CAN'T TEACH MY OLD HEART NEW TRICKS

Words by
JOHNNY MERCER

Music by
RICHARD A. WHITING

Can't teach my old heart new tricks,

it won't be-lieve that we're through, it keeps on beat-ing for

STOP, TIME

Lyrics by RICHARD MALTBY, Jr.
Music by DAVID SHIRE

Stop, Time - 3 - 1

© 1996 LONG POND MUSIC and DA-DI-DA MUSIC
All Rights for LONG POND MUSIC Administered by WB MUSIC CORP.
All Rights for DA-DI-DA MUSIC Administered by WARNER-TAMERLANE PUBLISHING CORP.
All Rights Reserved

UNWORTHY OF YOUR LOVE

Music and Lyrics by
STEPHEN SONDHEIM

Scene: The basement rec room in John Hinckley's house. *(Hinckley picks up his guitar and accompanies himself)*

HINCKLEY: Love, John.

Moderato (♩ = 112)
Poco rubato

HINCKLEY:

I am ____ noth-ing, ____ You are ____ wind and wa - ter and

Unworthy of Your Love - 8 - 1

© 1990, 1992 RILTING MUSIC, INC.
All rights administered by WB MUSIC CORP.
All Rights Reserved

WHAT MORE CAN I SAY?

Music and Lyrics by
WILLIAM FINN

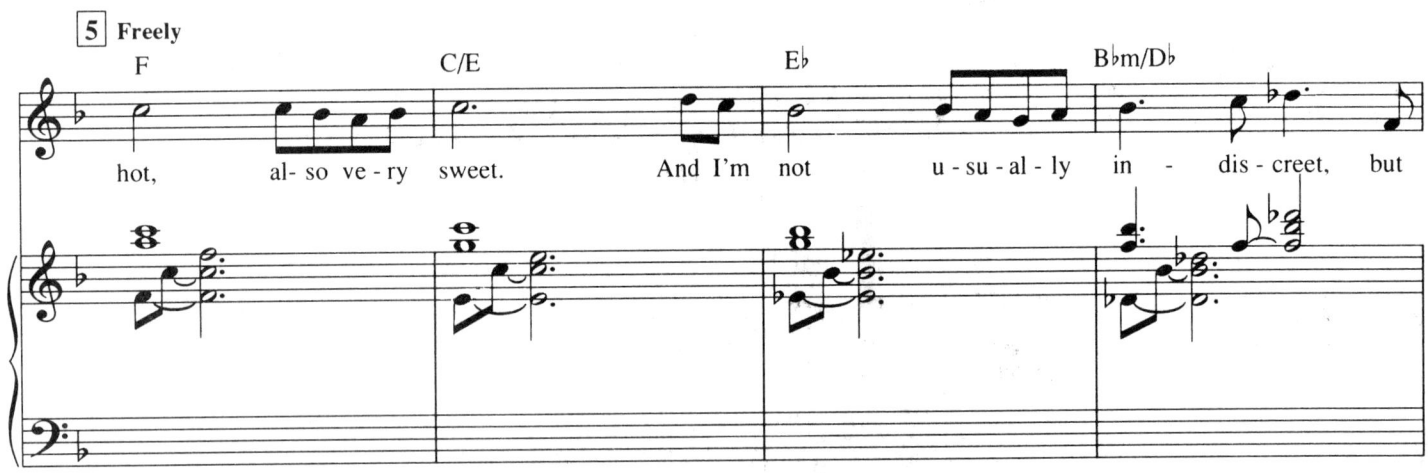

hot, al-so ve-ry sweet. And I'm not u-su-al-ly in-dis-creet, but

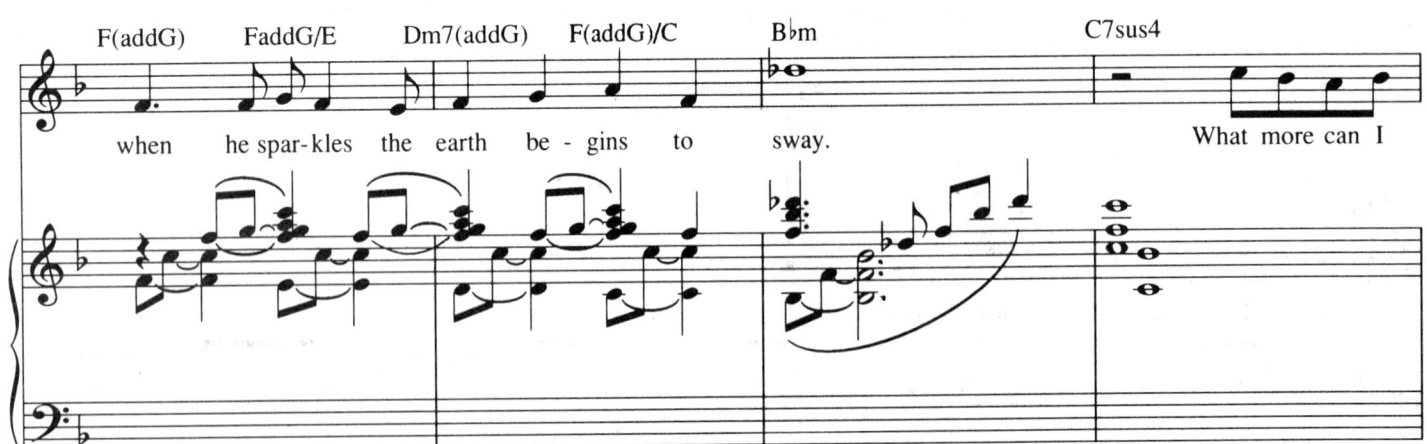

when he spar-kles the earth be-gins to sway. What more can I

13
F C/E E♭ B♭m/D♭ B♭m
say? How can I ex - press How con - fused am I by our hap - pi - ness. I
p
F(addG) F(addG)/E Dm7(addG) F(addG)/C B♭m
can't eat break - fast I can - not tie my shoe.
Csus4 F-5 F F-5 F
What more can I do?
p misterioso
23
F-5 F F-5 F Em7 C/E E♭+5 E♭6 Gsus4/D G/D
If I say I love him you might think my words come cheap.

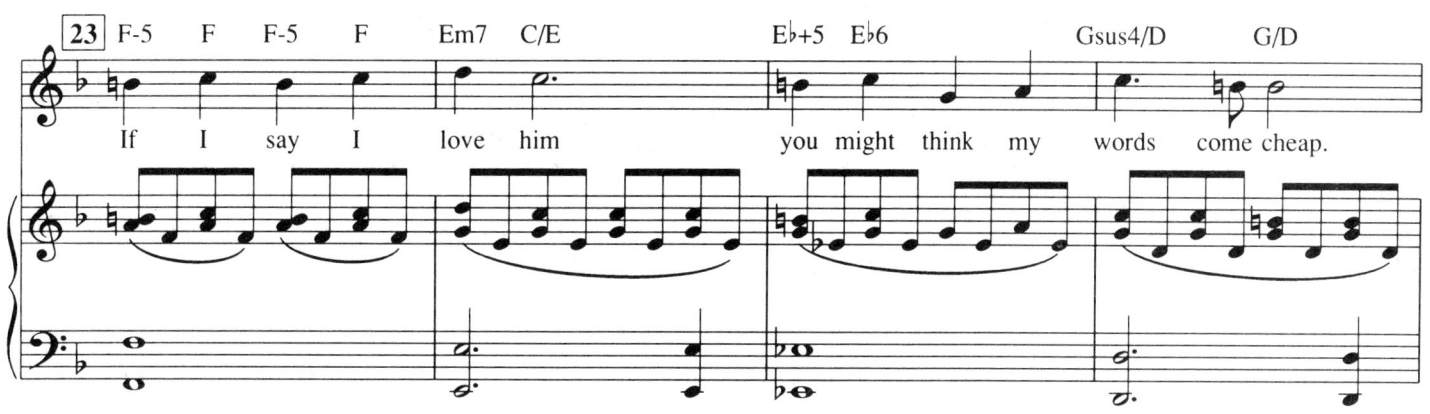

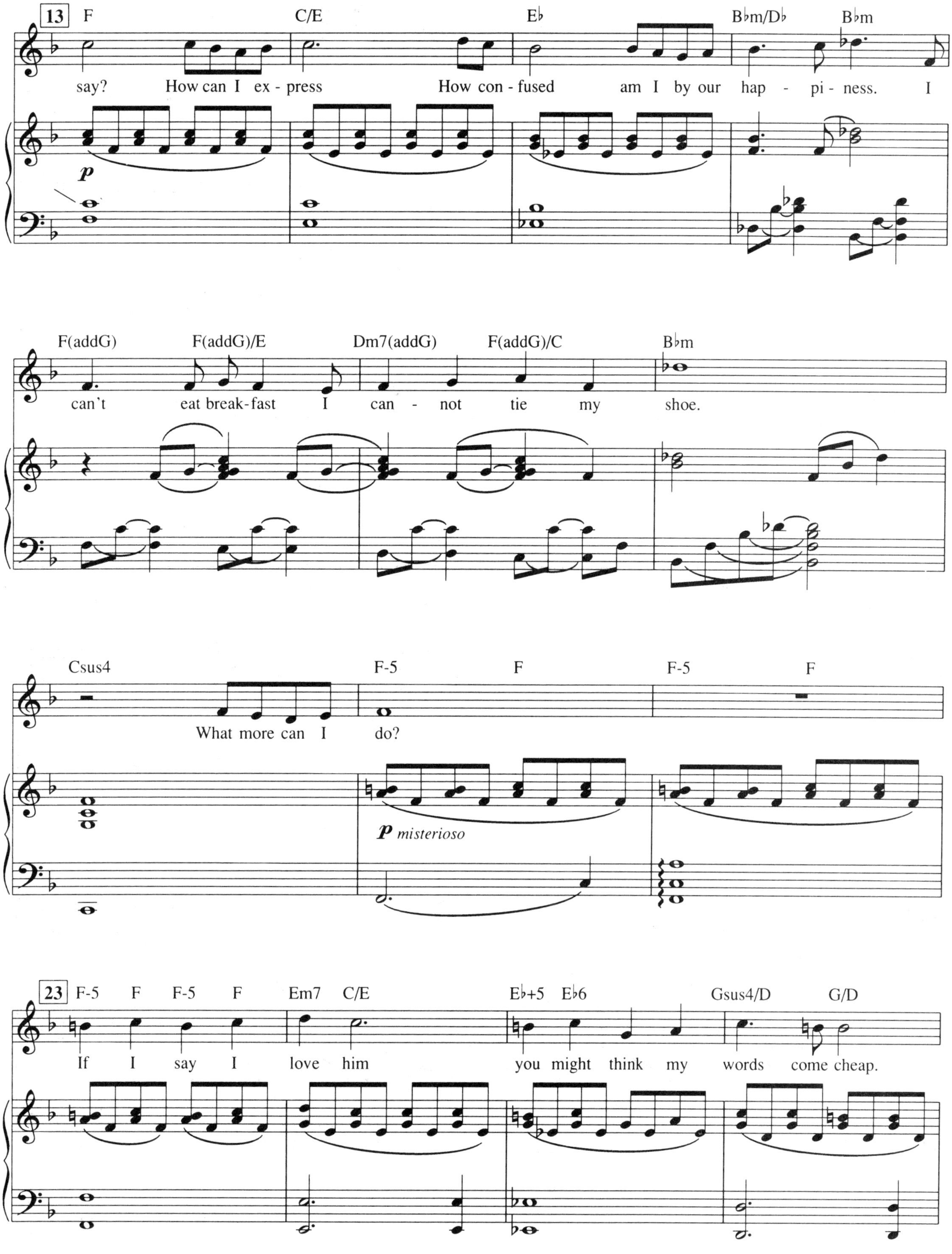

WHEN I LOOK AT YOU

Lyrics by
NAN KNIGHTON

Music by
FRANK WILDHORN

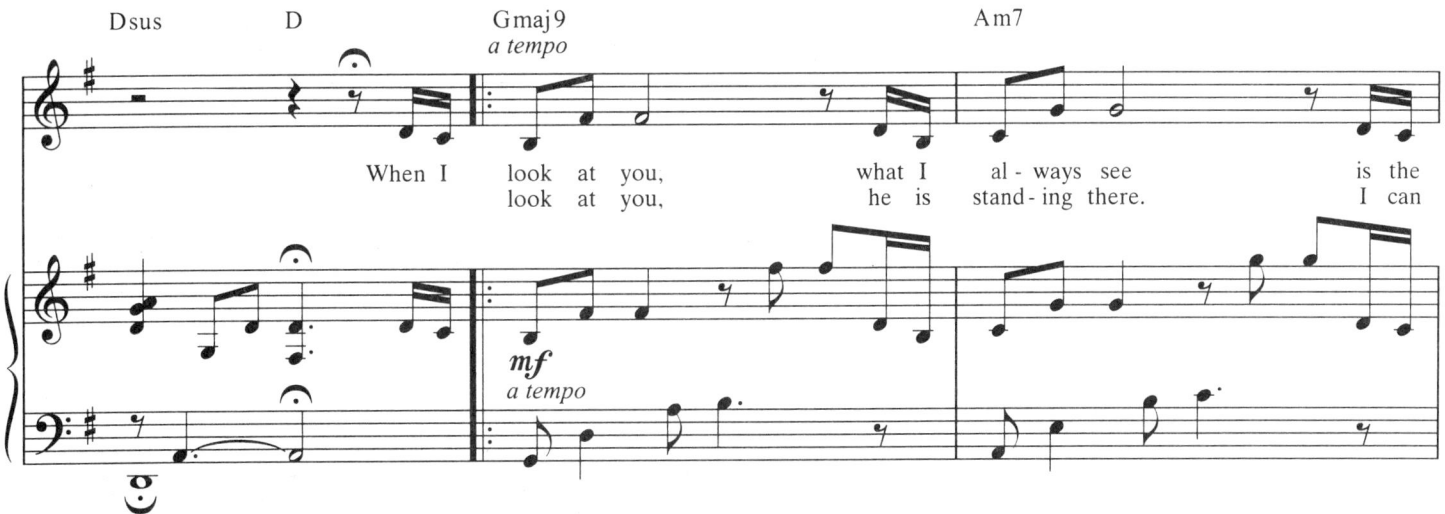

When I look at you, what I always see is the
look at you, he is standing there. I can

face of someone else who once belonged to me. Still I can hear him laugh, and
almost breathe him in like summer in the air. Why do you smile his smile? That

When I Look at You - 5 - 1

© 1992, 1998 WB MUSIC CORP., KNIGHT ERRANT MUSIC, SCARAMANGA MUSIC and BRONX FLASH MUSIC, INC.
All Rights on behalf of KNIGHT ERRANT MUSIC and SCARAMANGA MUSIC
Administered by WB MUSIC CORP.
All Rights Reserved including Public Performance for Profit

YOU'RE NOTHING WITHOUT ME

Music by
CY COLEMAN

Lyrics by
DAVID ZIPPEL

You're Nothing Without Me - 8 - 1

© 1989, 1990 NOTABLE MUSIC CO., INC.
All rights administered by WB MUSIC CORP.
All Rights Reserved

*Alternate lyrics for "YOU'RE NOTHING WITHOUT ME" (If alternate lyrics are used, begin song at this point.)
**Alternate lyrics for "I'M NOTHING WITHOUT YOU"

You're Nothing Without Me - 8 - 5

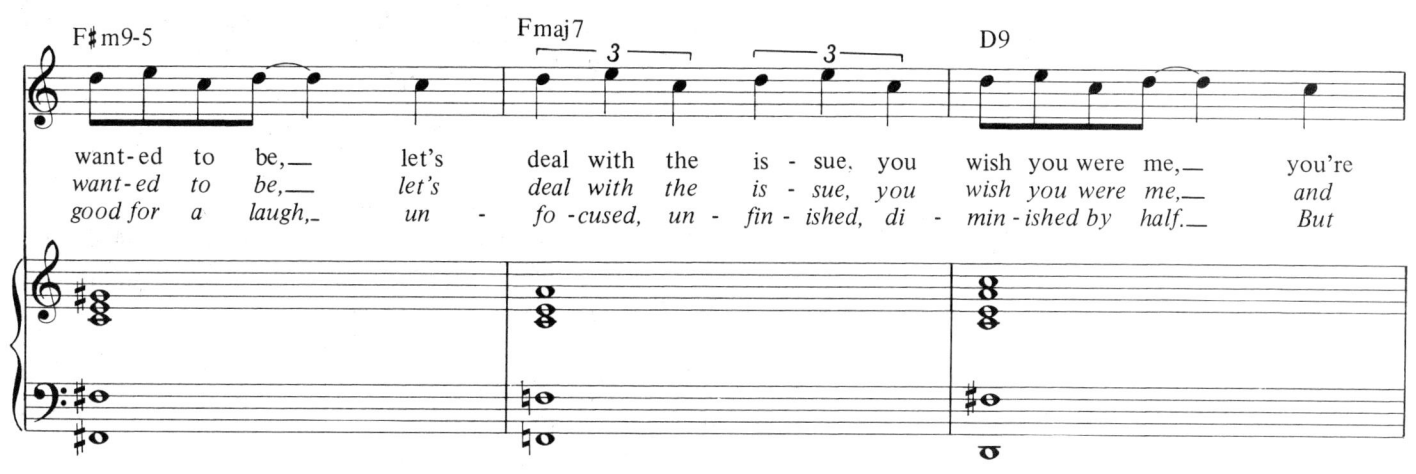
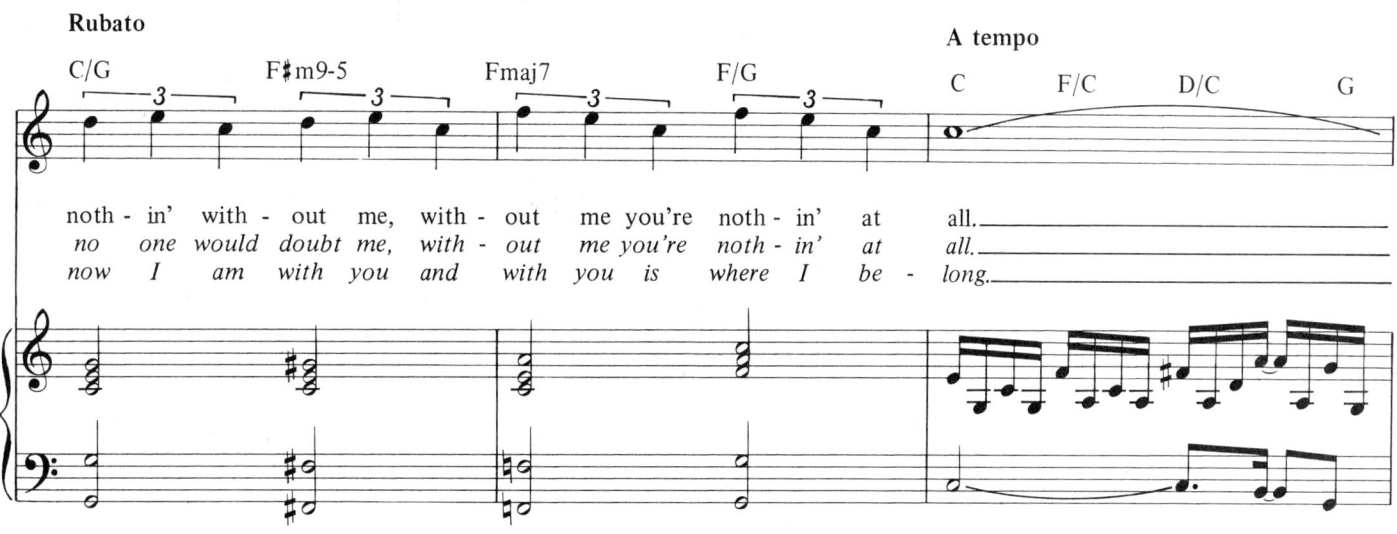

A WORLD WITHOUT YOU

Music and Lyrics by
STEPHEN SCHWARTZ

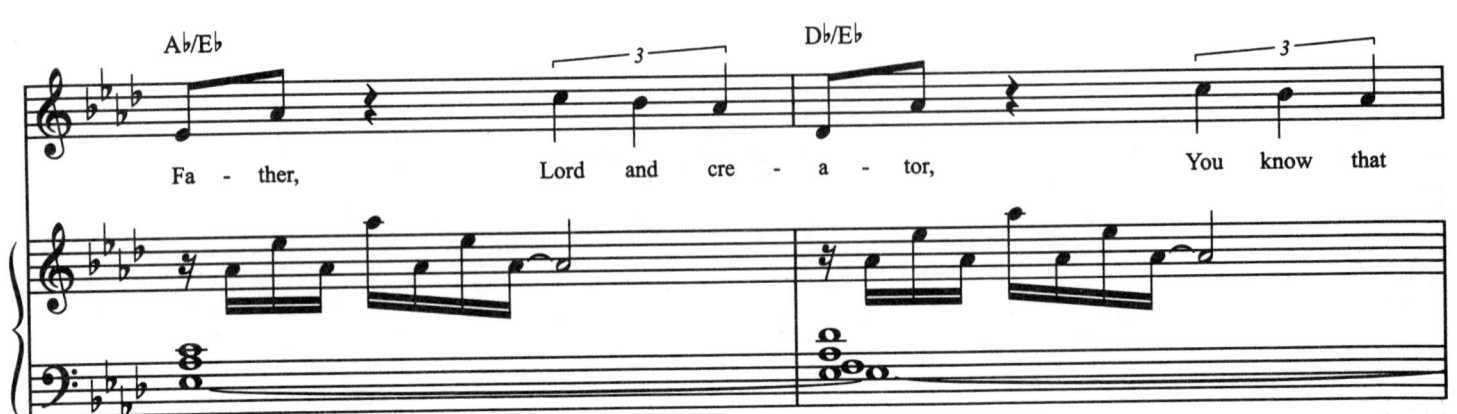

A World Without You - 6 - 1

© 1996 GREY DOG MUSIC
This Arrangement © 1999 GREY DOG MUSIC
All Rights Administered by WB MUSIC CORP.
All Rights Reserved including Public Performance for Profit

A World Without You - 6 - 5

THE OLDEST PROFESSION

Music by CY COLEMAN
Lyrics by IRA GASMAN

124

LATE NITE COMIC

Words and Music by
BRIAN GARI

Stay up at the din-er half the
Call the club and ask them for a
end up as the last one on the

night, try your best to get the new bit right. But the
spot, they say three A.M. is all we got. But you
show, sev-en heck-lers tell you where to go. And you

Late Nite Comic - 4 - 1

© 1978, 1987 TENACITY MUSIC and FOXBOROUGH MUSIC
This Arrangement ©1991 TENACITY MUSIC and FOXBOROUGH MUSIC
All Rights Reserved

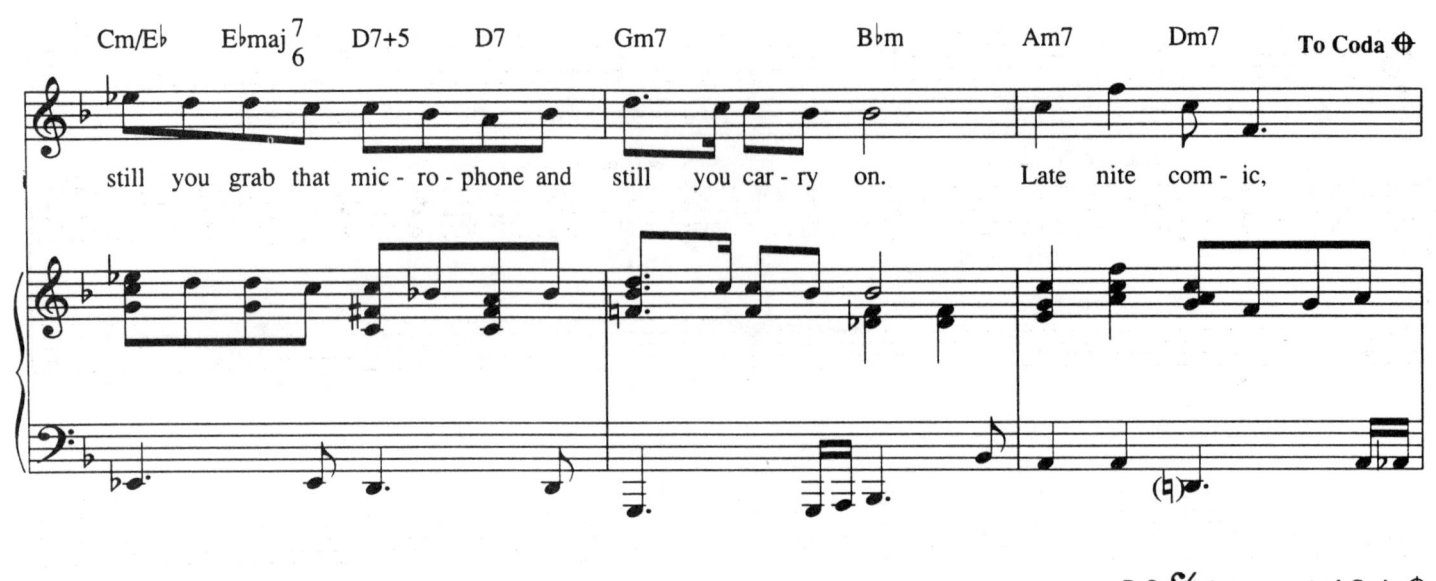

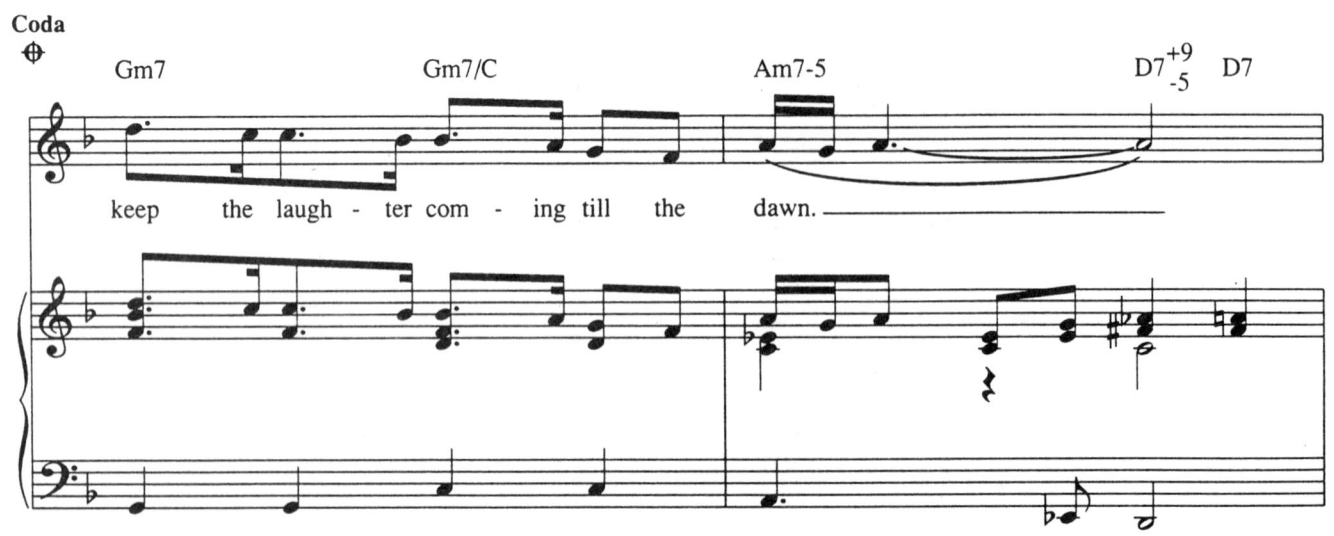

Reprise Lyric

I dream about her almost ev'ry night,
Try to tell myself that I'm all right
But I'm barely alive.
And sometimes I stay up all night and watch the day arrive
And fall asleep.

I walk around pretending I can walk,
Calling all my friends up just to talk
But it's always the same.
I do all the talking but I cannot say her name
Again just yet.

Late nite comic,
The girl I love is gone.
And what can bring her back again and make me carry on?
Late nite comic,
Maybe she'll be back before the dawn.

Fin'lly found the girl who made me laugh,
Someone made me whole instead of half
But it's over so soon.
I found her in the morning but she left by afternoon,
Now it's the night.

Late nite comic,
The girl I love is gone.
And what can bring her back again and make me carry on?
Late nite comic,
Maybe she'll be back before the dawn.
Late nite comic,
Late nite comic,
Late nite comic . . . carry on.

I'D RATHER BE SAILING

Words and Music by
WILLIAM FINN

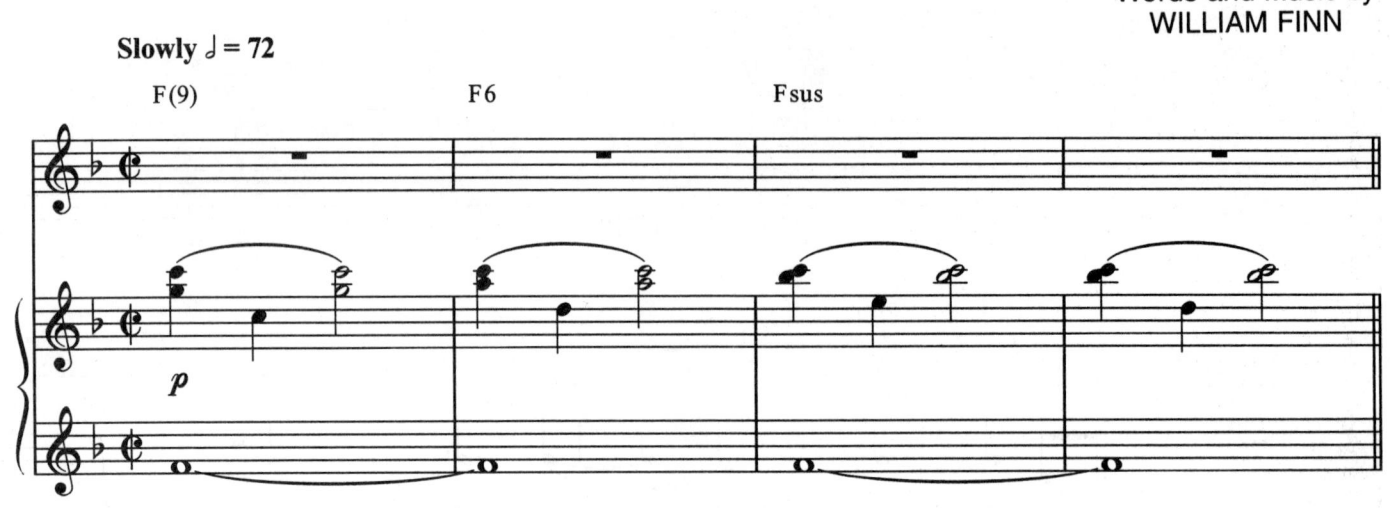

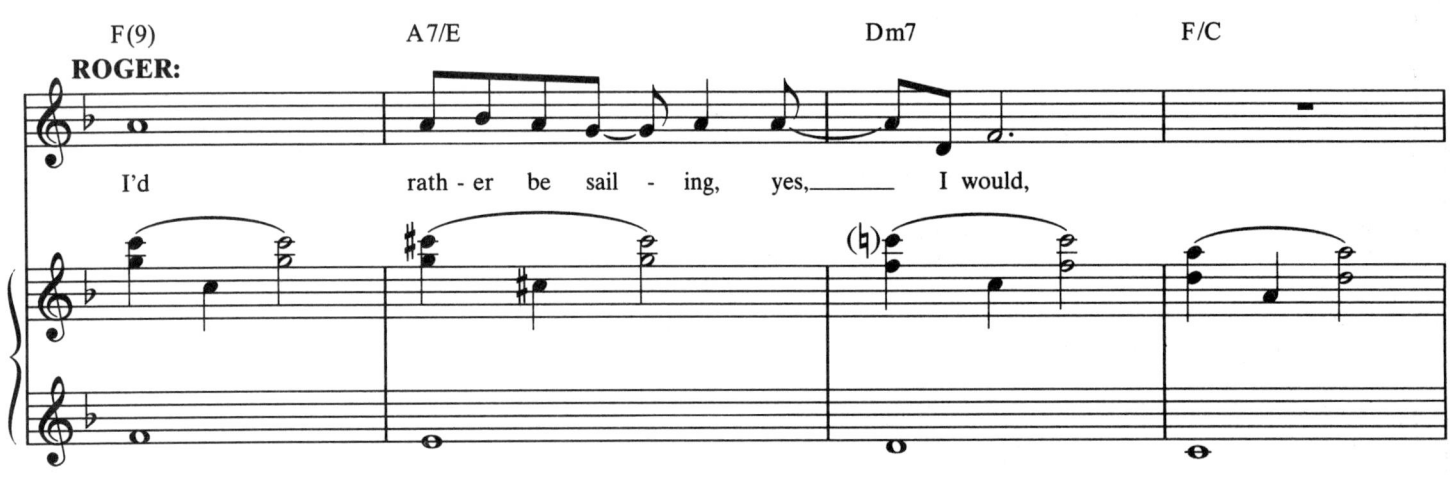

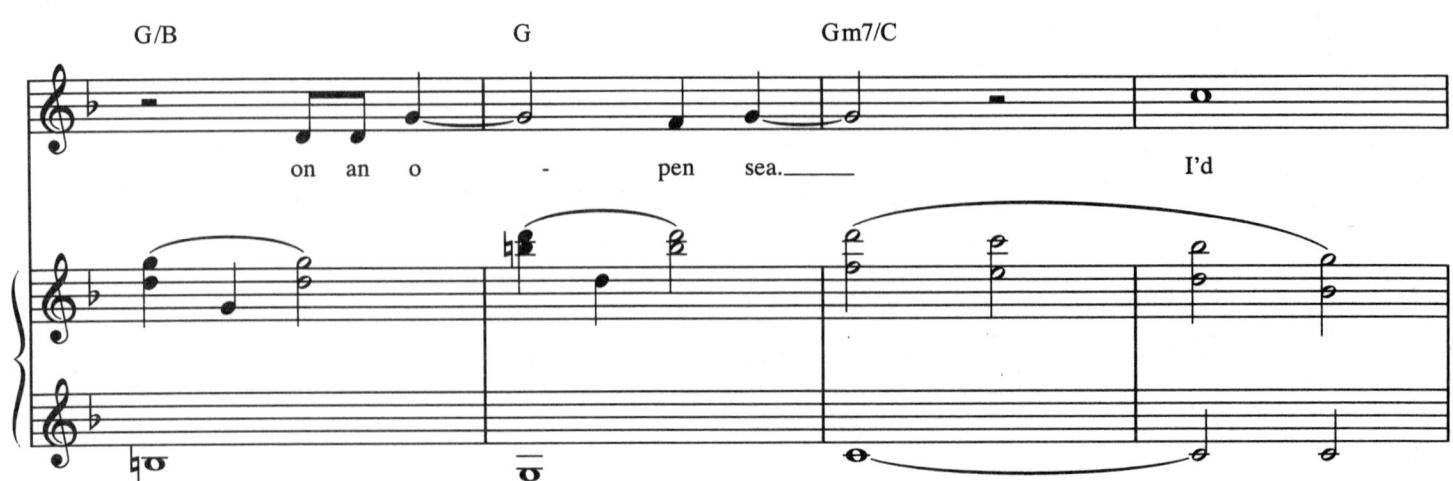

I'd Rather Be Sailing - 7 - 1

© 1998 WB MUSIC CORP. and IPSY PIPSY MUSIC
All Rights Administered by WB MUSIC CORP.
All Rights Reserved including Public Performance for Profit

MARRIED LIFE

Music by
CHARLES STROUSE

Lyrics by
RICHARD MALTBY, JR.

Life begins_____ after you're mar-ried.

Who's to say_____ the way it starts?

Married Life - 3 - 1

© 1992 CHARLES STROUSE PUBLICATIONS and LONG POND MUSIC
All Rights worldwide for CHARLES STROUSE PUBLICATIONS
Administered by HELENE BLUE MUSIQUE LTD.
All Rights for LONG POND MUSIC Administered by WB MUSIC CORP.
All Rights Reserved

YOU ARE MY HOME

Lyrics by
NAN KNIGHTON

Music by
FRANK WILDHORN

Moderate ballad ♩ = 72

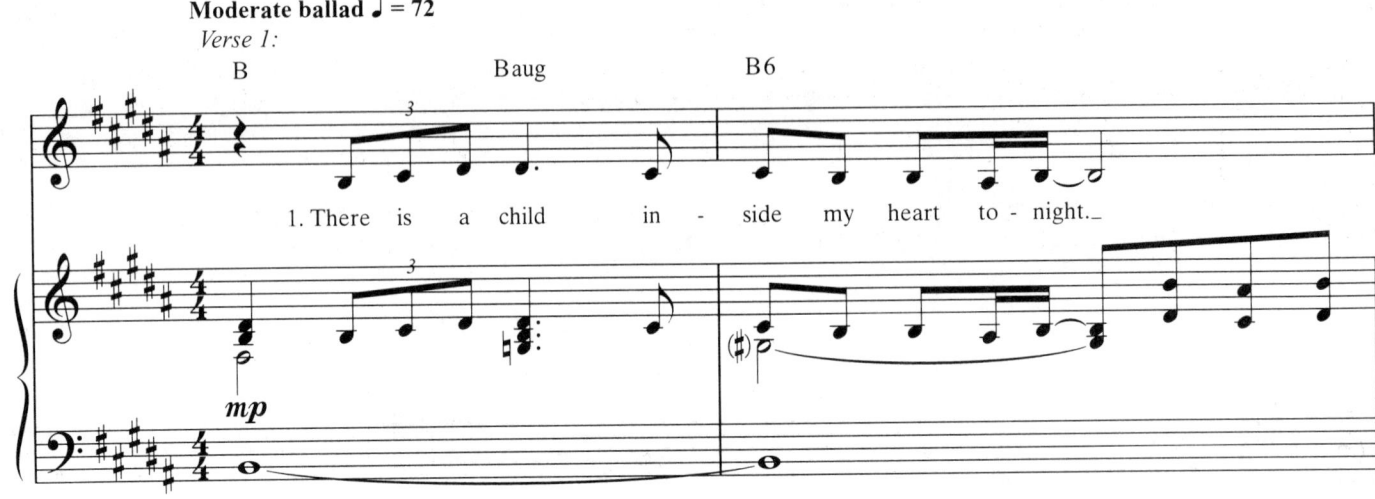

1. There is a child inside my heart tonight.

No one can see that child but you. If I hold on to you too

tight, you understand. You hold me too.

© 1991, 1998 WB MUSIC CORP, KNIGHT ERRANT MUSIC,
SCARAMANGA MUSIC and BRONX FLASH MUSIC, INC.
All Rights on behalf of KNIGHT ERRANT MUSIC and SCARAMANGA MUSIC
Administered by WB MUSIC CORP.
All Rights Reserved including Public Performance for Profit

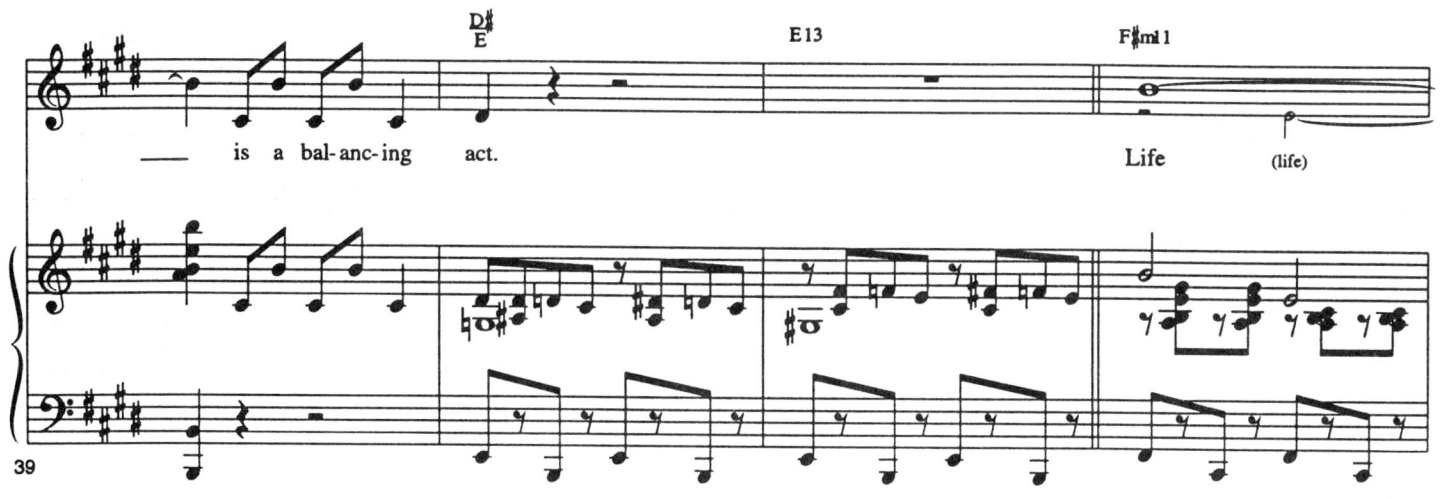

Life Is a Balancing Act - 4 - 4

WHEELS OF A DREAM

Lyrics by
LYNN AHRENS

Music by
STEPHEN FLAHERTY

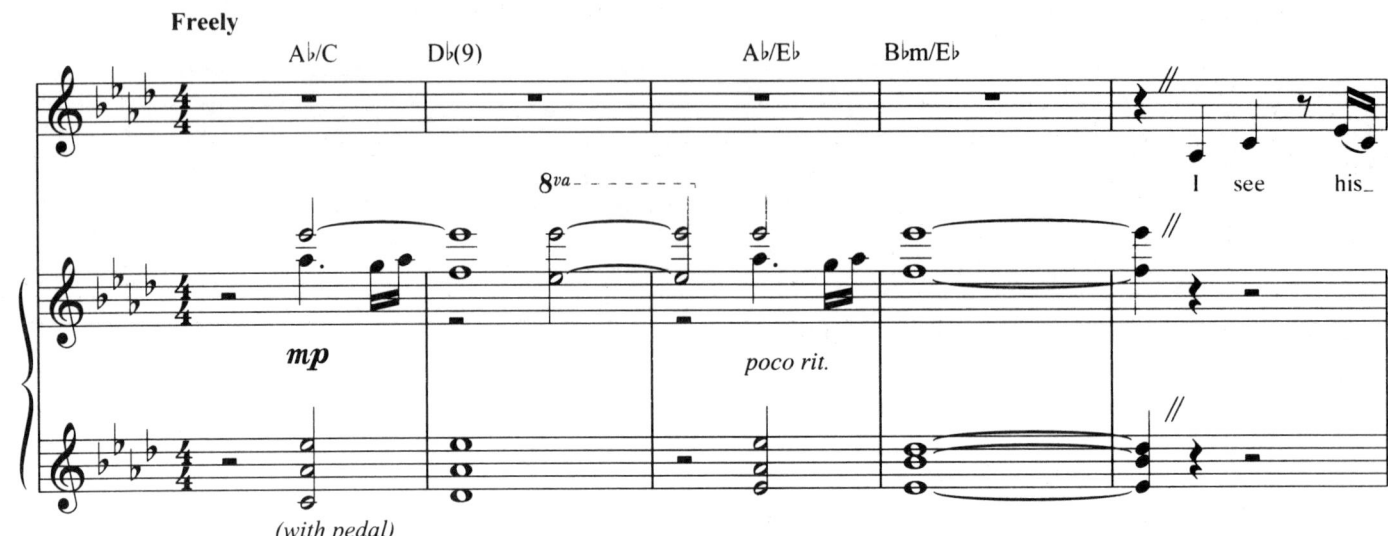
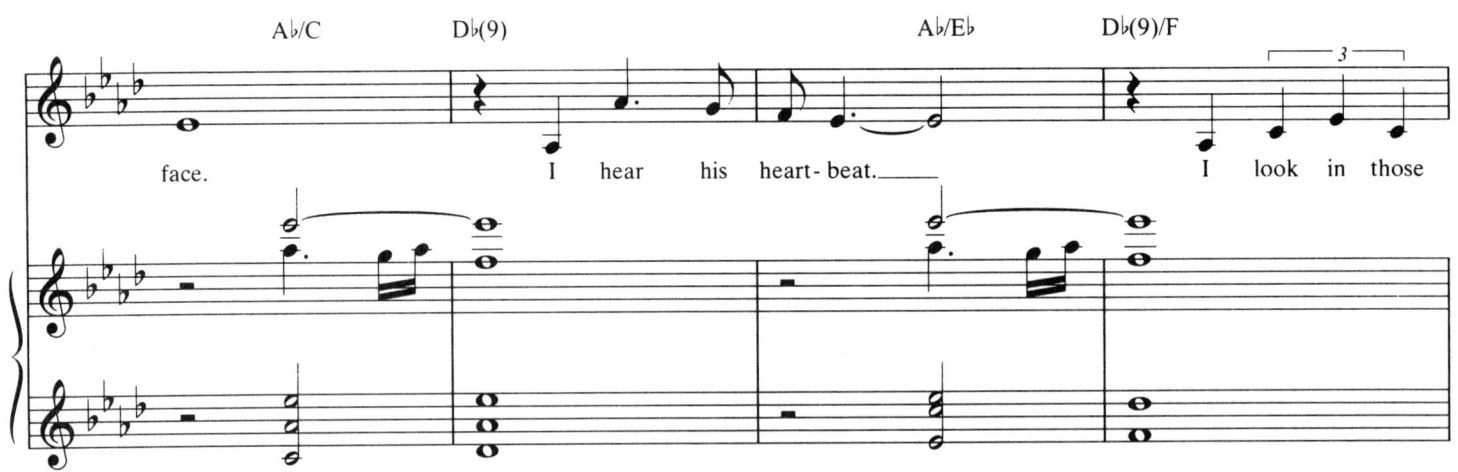
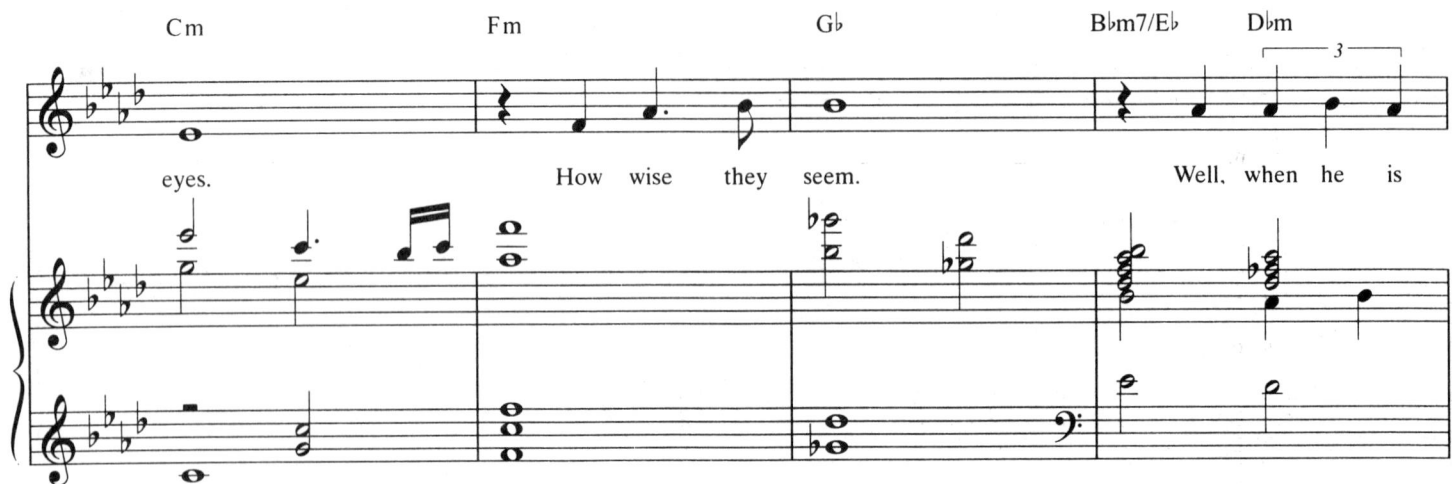

© 1996, 1997 WB MUSIC CORP., PEN AND PERSEVERANCE and Hillsdale Music, INC.
All Rights Administered by WB MUSIC CORP.
All Rights Reserved including Public Performance for Profit

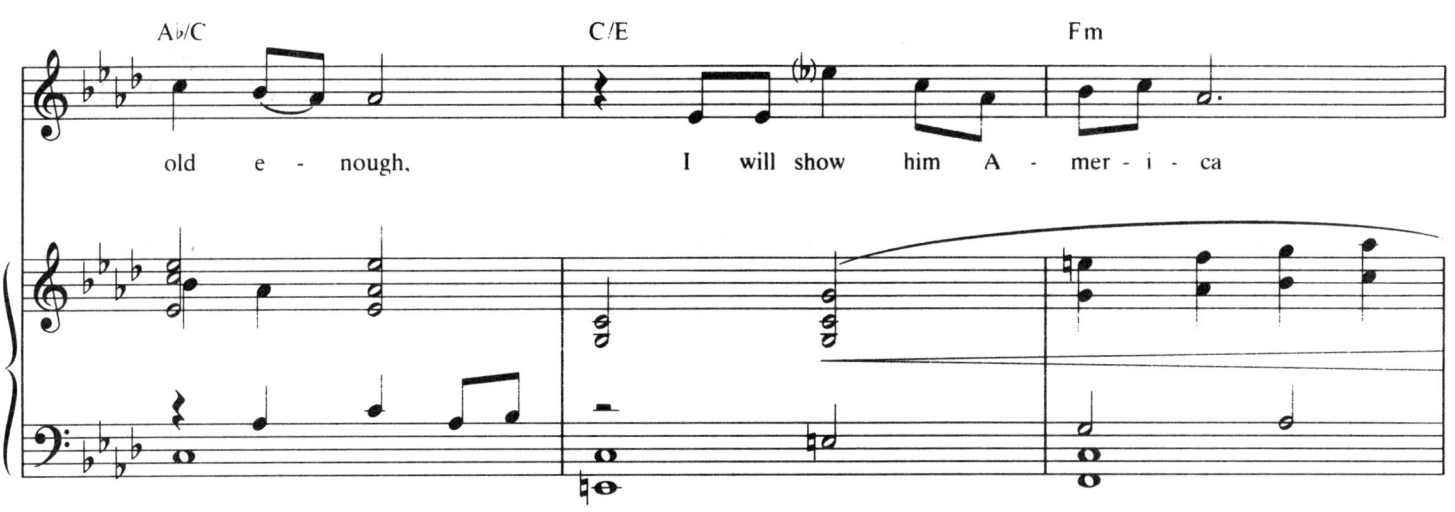
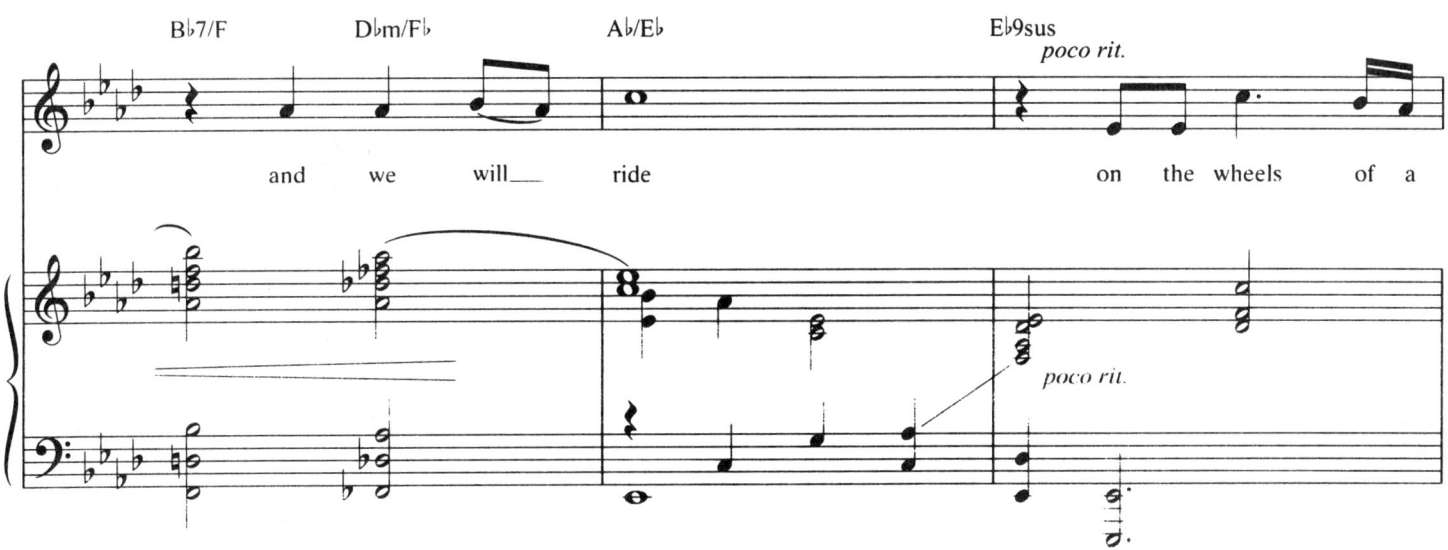

170

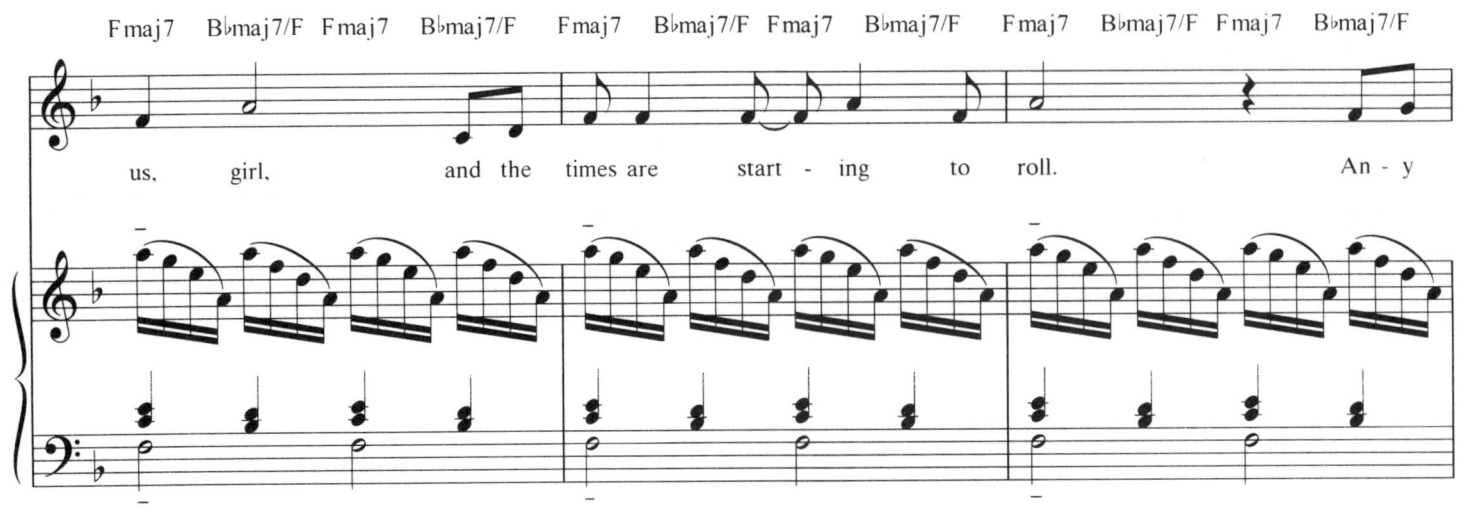

us, girl, and the times are start-ing to roll. An-y

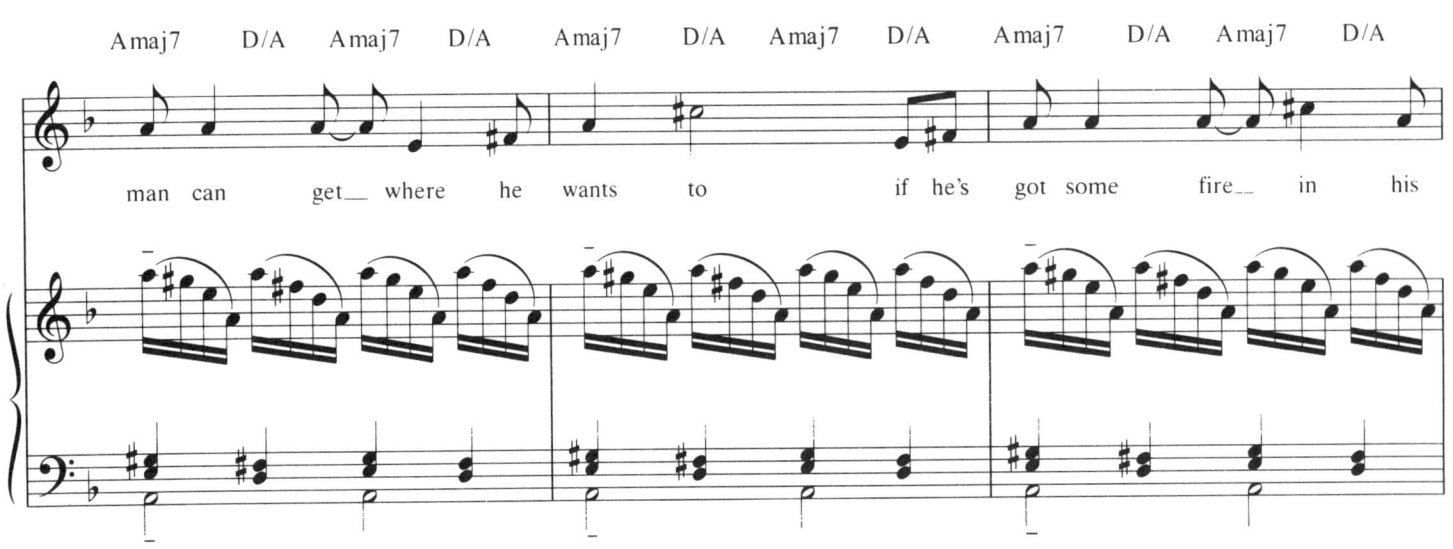

man can get where he wants to if he's got some fire in his

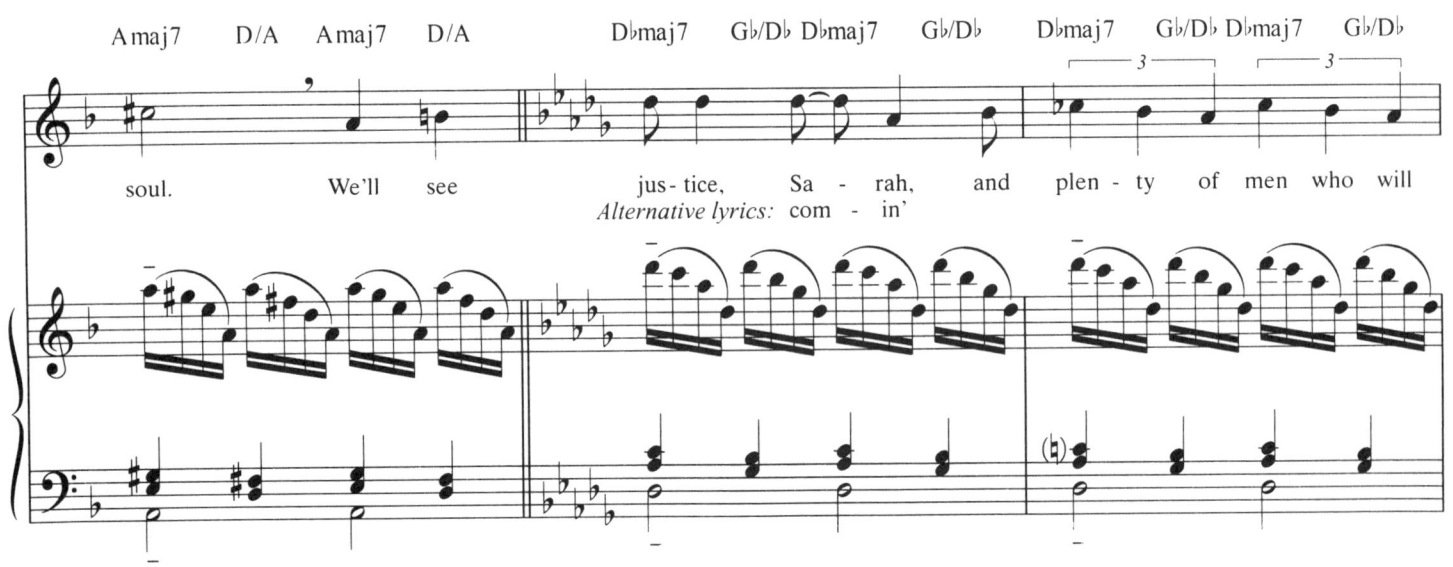

soul. We'll see jus-tice, Sa-rah, and plen-ty of men who will
Alternative lyrics: com - in'

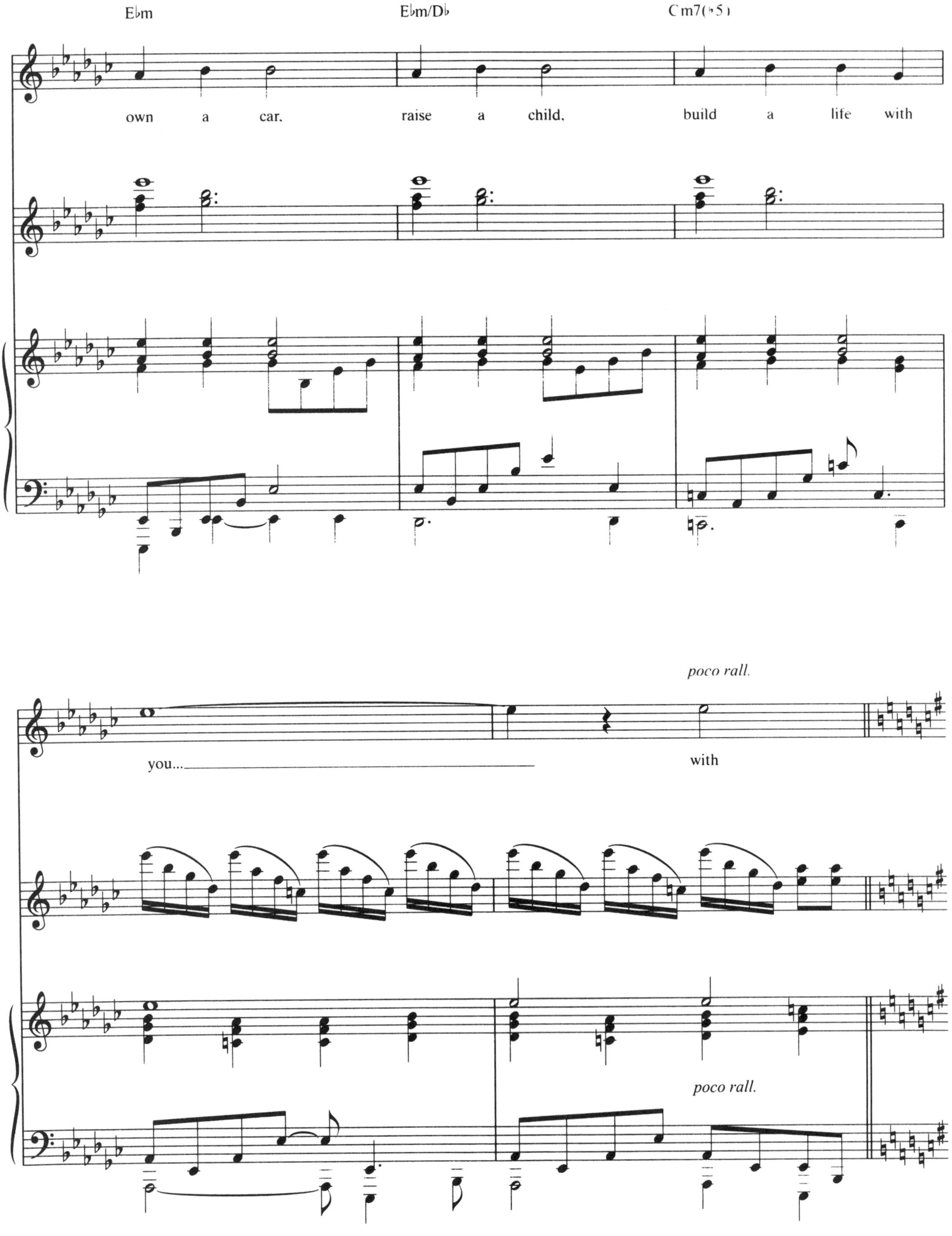
E♭m
E♭m/D♭
Cm7(♭5)
own a car,
raise a child,
build a life with
you...
poco rall.
with
poco rall.

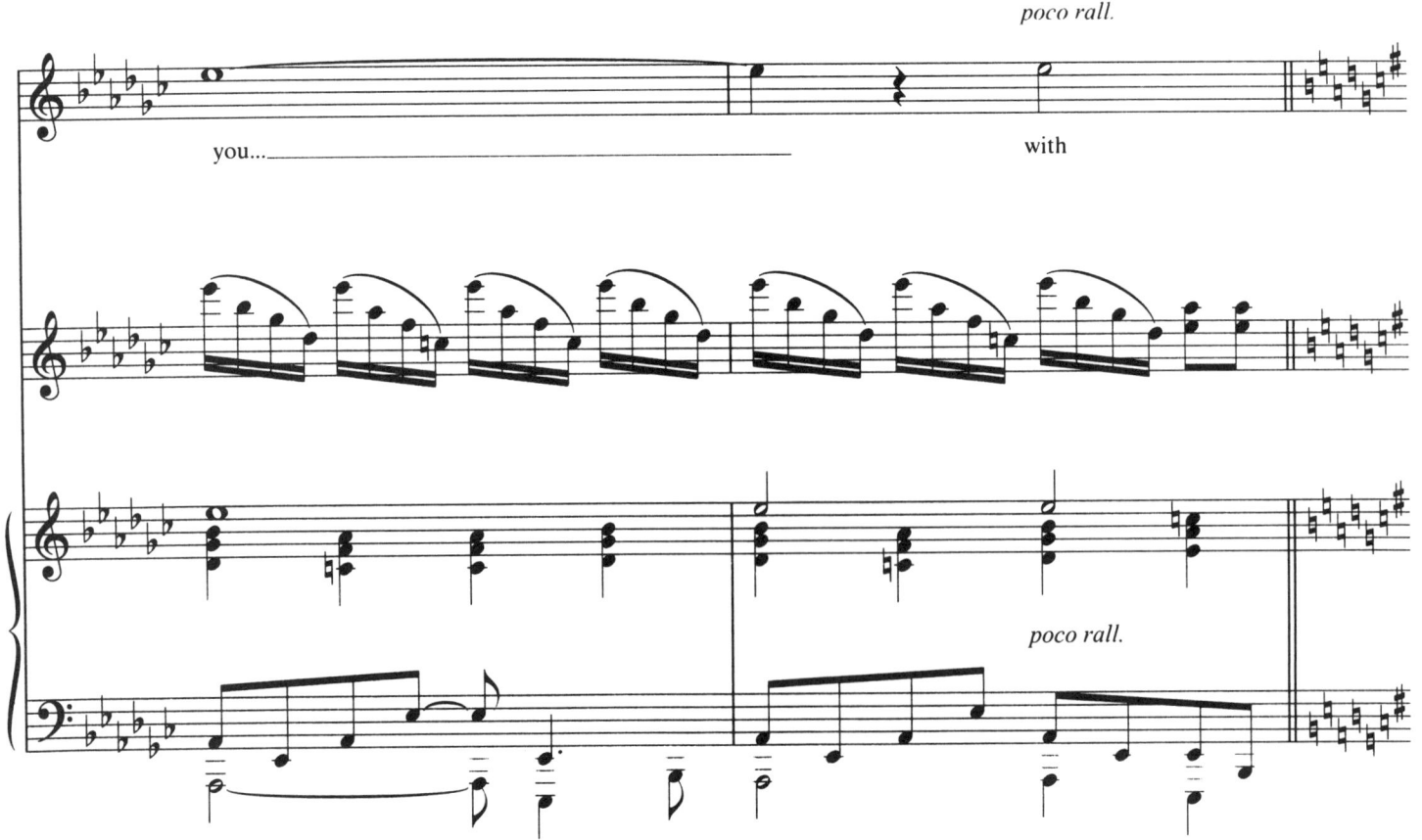

WAY BACK TO PARADISE

Words and Music by
MICHAEL JOHN LaCHIUSA

Moderato

MARIE CHRISTINE:

We are ruled by our brothers. We are ruled by our husbands. We

jump at the voices of our masters and do as they say. We are

178

THE SMASH BROADWAY COLLECTION
100 Great Songs of the Century

Piano/Vocal/Chords
(MFM0001)

This comprehensive collection includes historical notes and rare photos from 40 Broadway hits, *including:*

ANNIE	**GIRL CRAZY**	**PORGY AND BESS**®
BRIGADOON	**HAIR**	**PROMISES, PROMISES**
BYE BYE BIRDIE	**JESUS CHRIST SUPERSTAR**	**RAGTIME**
DAMN YANKEES	**A LITTLE NIGHT MUSIC**	**THE SCARLET PIMPERNEL**
EVITA	**LITTLE SHOP OF HORRORS**	**SHOWBOAT**
FIDDLER ON THE ROOF	**OF THEE I SING**	**SWEENEY TODD**
FOSSE	**ON THE TOWN**	**SWEET CHARITY**
42ND STREET	**THE PAJAMA GAME**	**VICTOR/VICTORIA**
FUNNY FACE	**PAL JOEY**	**THE WIZ**

Song highlights are:

ALL THE THINGS YOU ARE • ALMOST LIKE BEING IN LOVE • BE OUR GUEST • BEAUTY AND THE BEAST • BIG SPENDER • BILL • DON'T CRY FOR ME ARGENTINA • GOOD MORNING STARSHINE • HEART • HEY, LOOK ME OVER • I DON'T KNOW HOW TO LOVE HIM • I GET A KICK OUT OF YOU • IF I WERE A RICH MAN • A LOT OF LIVIN' TO DO • LUCKY TO BE ME • MACK THE KNIFE • MAKE BELIEVE • MR. BOJANGLES • MY FUNNY VALENTINE • OL' MAN RIVER • ON A CLEAR DAY (YOU CAN SEE FOREVER) • PUT ON A HAPPY FACE • SEND IN THE CLOWNS • SMOKE GETS IN YOUR EYES • STEAM HEAT • SUMMERTIME • SUNRISE, SUNSET • SUPERSTAR • TO LIFE • TOMORROW • WHEELS OF A DREAM.

Plus many, many more classics!

Available from your local music store

From the stage to the page

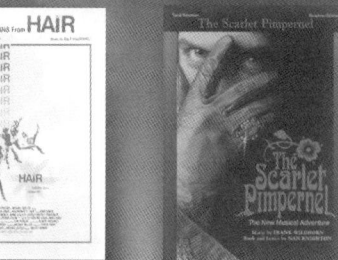

Warner Bros. Publications has the

Best of Broadway